1989 Ed.

Parker's Modern Conveyancing Precedents

Parker's
Modern Conveyancing Precedents

Second edition

Editor

Eric Taylor LLM
Solicitor

Assistant Editor

J M McKean MA
Solicitor

Consultant Editor

J E Adams LLB
Solicitor
Emeritus Professor of Law
Queen Mary College
University of London

Butterworths
London and Edinburgh
1989

United Kingdom	Butterworth & Co (Publishers) Ltd 88 Kingsway, LONDON WC2B 6AB and 4 Hill Street, EDINBURGH EH2 3JZ
Australia	Butterworths Pty Ltd, SYDNEY, MELBOURNE, BRISBANE, ADELAIDE, PERTH, CANBERRA and HOBART
Canada	Butterworths Canada Ltd, TORONTO and VANCOUVER
Ireland	Butterworth (Ireland) Ltd, DUBLIN
Malaysia	Malayan Law Journal Pte Ltd, KUALA LUMPUR
New Zealand	Butterworths of New Zealand Ltd, WELLINGTON and AUCKLAND
Singapore	Butterworth & Co (Asia) Pte Ltd, SINGAPORE
USA	Butterworths Legal Publishers, ST PAUL, Minnesota, SEATTLE, Washington, BOSTON, Massachusetts, AUSTIN, Texas and D & S Publishers, CLEARWATER, Florida

A CIP Catalogue record for this book is available from the British Library.

ISBN 0 406 33451 X

Printed and bound in Great Britain by Bookcraft (Bath) Ltd

Preface

The publication of *Modern Conveyancing Precedents* in 1964 was the first serious attempt to use plain English when drafting legal documents. It encouraged others, in particular building societies, to follow suit. During the past 20 years, many government departments and large institutions have made conscious efforts to make the documents they create more intelligible to the general public. I should like to think that the existence of Parker's first edition has, to some extent, been responsible for this.

The editors of the second edition have made some changes in the wording of precedents but they have throughout tried to maintain the principles of the first edition. There have been changes in the contents of the book arising from changes in the law and the needs of practitioners. For example, the section on rentcharges has been pruned because it is no longer possible to create new rentcharges; the section headed 'individual owners' has been considerably expanded; a new section relating to transfers between husband and wife (or, more particularly, between former spouses) has been introduced and the section on mortgages has been expanded. A number of precedents which were little used in practice have been omitted. The precedents in the first edition relating to leases and underleases have also been omitted. They were really estate development precedents. The present editors originally intended to include a new section devoted to estate development but, reluctantly, abandoned this idea for two reasons. Firstly, it became clear that it would be difficult to produce precedents that would cover the requirements of the various forms of estate development and, secondly, the precedents in the first edition were not much used because, I think, builders' solicitors were unwilling to abandon the traditional precedents used by their firms over the years which they felt had stood the test of time. Of the six contributors to the first edition, only the present editors are alive and still practising as solicitors but we do not forget the contribution to the 1964 edition of the other three and we acknowledge our indebtedness to them for their earlier work.

It would be remiss of us not to acknowledge the patience shown by the staff of Messrs Butterworths and the help they have given. In particular, they have indulged the editors' whim to have 'sidenotes' instead of 'footnotes' which, incidentally, gives the user space, adjacent to the precedent, for his own annotations.

Eric Taylor
Middleton
June 1989

Contents

Part 3 Mortgages vacating receipts and property subject to mortgages

Editor's Notes

Adapted from the notes of the Editor of the first edition in 1964, Mr Anthony Parker

For some time there has been discussion among lawyers about making conveyancing documents more easily understood by the clients who sign them. Most views expressed fall between two extremes.

The extreme on one side holds that legal documents are communications between one lawyer and another lawyer, that they are technical communications, that it is not necessary or convenient for the public to understand them and that the traditional documents are suitable for the purpose for which they are intended. This view may possibly carry more weight in the case of those forensic documents which are signed by the lawyer and not by the client, yet even in such cases I should have thought it unwise to treat the understanding of the client as beneath notice. Conveyancing documents are signed by clients and it seems wrong that people should be required to sign a document which is incomprehensible to them; the solicitor may explain the meaning, as though the document were written in a foreign language, but this wastes time and may not be freely accepted by the client. I do not suggest that clients must be able to understand the few technical expressions which are necessary for full legal effect; for instance clients quite happily accept that the expression 'beneficial owner' is legal shorthand for certain covenants for title. Even on the basis that a conveyancing document is comparable with a medical prescription, which is a communication from doctor to chemist direct, can the extremists maintain that the traditional wording is satisfactory as between lawyer and lawyer?

The extreme from the opposite view is that all formal wording is useless and should be swept aside, and that it should be stated in a few sentences that A transfers the property to B, along the lines of a transfer of land registered in the Land Registry. While I have sympathy with this, I cannot agree that it is possible to carry it out in the case of unregistered land without a new Act of Parliament. All that is within our power is to express the intentions of clients in a manner which is as clear and concise as possible and which is effective according to present legislation.

Tautology makes lawyers appear ridiculous. It provokes derision from the educated, and stupefies the uneducated; it is not good English, and it is not legally necessary. Some of the traditional expressions appear to have been written, not by a worldy lawyer, but by an old woman in a state of nervous apprehension. In preparing these new precedents, I and my collaborators have steered a course between the two extreme views. It is not suggested that a compromise is always the ideal policy, yet in this particular instance a compromise seems to be better and more practical than either of the extremes.

The objects

The main objects have been:

1. To produce the full legal effect intended.
2. To make the documents more comprehensible to clients, and thus to assist in relations between solicitors and the public.
3. To avoid the abuse of the English language found in the traditional precedents.
4. To avoid the confusion of thought and expression found in some of the traditional precedents.
5. To make the documents shorter, and so to save time and money.

Sometimes part of the draft (for example the description of the property) must be composed by the conveyancer. I hope that those conveyancers who approve our ideas will, when it is their turn to devise part of the document, follow the principles which we suggest and make the draft shorter, easier to check and to copy, and easier for clients to follow.

Drafting conveyancing documents

Description of properties

Where there is a postal address this should be given exactly as if addressing a letter and, where possible, the postcode should be included. Once a place has been mentioned there is no need afterwards to refer to it as 'aforesaid'. It follows that the reference is to the same place, unless the contrary is indicated.

Often plans on a conveyance are unsatisfactory. Often they are small and badly copied. Sometimes they are out of date. They are described as being 'for identification purposes only', yet plans which are properly so described are almost useless. Whenever possible a scale plan should be prepared by a surveyor.

Punctuation

The system of punctuation for legal documents has become entirely confused; perhaps it would be better expressed as "a system of lack of punctuation". The refusal to use a comma has reached such fantastic lengths that we often read this sort of thing:

> 'By a Conveyance dated   and made between John Williams Vaughan Jones Richards and Thomas Richards of the one part and Ivan Williams Jones Thomas Hughes Richard Vernon and Richard Simpson of the other part . . .'

No one can ascertain which are the surnames or how many people are named. I believe that lawyers originally feared commas because of the proposition that one should not allow the sense of what one writes to depend on punctuation. That is sound, but it does not logically follow that we must dispense with all punctuation. To accept the statement that a country's exports should not depend on tin tacks does not mean that no tin tacks should be exported.

It is important that sentences should not be constructed in a fashion so tangled that the meaning is altered if a punctuation mark is omitted, yet if proper attention is given to the construction of sentences and they are fairly short, there should be no difficulty.

Punctuation should be used sparingly but it need not be completely avoided because there are times where it creates order out of a jumble of words or names but on no account should commas be used as a means of creating a maze of phrases in one sentence.

Capital initial letters

The use of initial capital letters should be governed by the ordinary rules of prose composition, except that it is convenient to use a capital initial to identify a 'shorthand term' (eg 'the Vendor') where this expression has been established earlier in the document.

Recitals

It is unsatisfactory to rely on the abstract of title as the sole means of recording important information, for it is not sufficiently robust, and is not signed by the vendor. On the other hand there is no need to employ the traditional preamble in the conveyance about the title in by-gone years. The facts recited should be limited to the minumum. See, for example, Precedents 20 and 39.

Interpretation clauses

The useful construction clause in LPA 1925, s 61 is often overlooked. It can save a lot of involved provisions.

Part 1   Freeholds

A   Individual Owners

1

Conveyance of a single house[1]

This Conveyance dated
is made between:
(1) the Vendor
(2) the Purchaser

1 The Vendor acknowledges the receipt from the Purchaser of
£   the purchase price of the property described in the schedule
('the Property').

2 The Vendor as beneficial owner conveys to the Purchaser the fee
simple estate in the Property.

3 The Property is subject to such covenants and restrictions contained
in a conveyance dated *etc* as are still effective and the Purchaser
covenants with the Vendor to indemnify him against liability resulting
from any future breach or non-observance of those covenants.

Certificate of value (if applicable)

Schedule

Description of Property

1   This precedent is only included because it is suitable for reproduction as a proforma conveyance. Even then it has limited application. Our original intention was to produce a number of proforma conveyances but the increased use of word processors has reduced the advantages of solicitors maintaining a stock of proformas.

2

Conveyance of a single house where an earlier deed contains an adequate description of the property

This Conveyance dated
is made between:
(1) the Vendor
(2) the Purchaser

1 The Vendor acknowledges the receipt from the Purchaser of £   the purchase price of the land and house known as [*postal address*] ('the Property') which is fully described in a conveyance dated *etc.*

2 The Vendor as beneficial owner conveys to the Purchaser the fee simple estate in the Property.

Add any appropriate standard clauses

Certificate of value (if applicable)

3

Conveyance of a single house subject to existing restrictive covenants

This Coveyance dated
is made between:
(1) the Vendor
(2) the Purchaser

1   The Vendor acknowledges the receipt from the Purchaser of £   the purchase price of the land and house known as [*postal address*] ('the Property') which is fully described in a conveyance dated *etc*.

2   The Vendor as beneficial owner conveys to the Purchaser the fee simple estate in the Property.

3   The Property is subject to such covenants and restrictions contained in a conveyance dated *etc* as are still effective.

4   The Purchaser covenants with the Vendor to indemnify the Vendor against liability resulting from any future breach or non-observance of the covenants referred to in clause 3.[1]

Add any appropriate standard clauses

Certificate of value (if applicable)

1   See Standard Clauses pp 292ff for different forms of covenant for indemnity.

4

Conveyance of one of a pair of semi-detached houses owned by the vendor[1]

This Conveyance dated
is made between:
(1) the Vendor
(2) the Purchaser

1 The Vendor acknowledges the receipt from the Purchaser of £   the purchase price of the land and house known as [*postal address*] ('the Property Conveyed') which is fully described in the first schedule.

2 The Vendor as beneficial owner conveys to the Purchaser the fee simple estate in the Property Conveyed.

3 The parties declare that:

(a) any wall fence or hedge separating the Property Conveyed from the adjoining land and house known as [*postal address*] ('the Retained Premises') shall be a party structure to be repaired and maintained at the equally shared expense of its owners;[2]

(b) any sewers drains electricity cables gas pipes gutters downspouts and similar conduits serving both the Property Conveyed and the Retained Premises shall continue to be used as they were prior to the date of this deed [and shall be repaired and maintained at the equally shared expense of the owners of the Property Conveyed and the Retained Premises];[2]

(c) no rights of way over the Retained Premises shall be implied in this deed;[3]

(d) section 62 of the Law of Property Act 1925 shall not apply to this deed.[3]

4 The Vendor undertakes to keep safe the documents listed in the second schedule and acknowledges the right of the Purchaser to their production and to the supply of copies.

Add any appropriate standard clauses

Certificate of value (if applicable)

First Schedule
The land and house known as [*postal address*] but except and reserved from this conveyance any easement quasi-easement or right that prior to the date of this deed was enjoyed by the Vendor for the benefit of the

1   Please refer to the Appendix (pp 299ff) for observations of general application to sales-off.

2   Most draftsmen make provision for the cost of repairing and maintaining party structures to be borne by the parties in equal shares, as in the precedent. The cost of rebuilding, say, a party wall could be expensive. Moreover, neither party is likely to undertake the work without the other contributing to its cost. The same considerations do not apply to conduits. Some draftsmen prefer to make no provision for their maintenance, relying on the fact that the owner of each house is likely to undertake the repair of conduits on or under his own property and that, in many cases, it is hardly worth seeking a contribution. Different considerations would apply however to, say, a private sewer serving the two houses. In some circumstances, it may be proper to provide for the contribution to repairs to be in unequal shares. Whenever possible, however, it is preferable to define the contribution of the parties rather than make provision for the payment of a 'fair proportion of the cost' which can be a fruitful source of dispute in the future.

3   It is likely that this provision will require to be adapted to the circumstances. It has been inserted to remind the draftsman of the need to give consideration to these matters. See Appendix pp 299ff.

Retained Premises and which continues to be necessary to the reasonable enjoyment of the Retained Premises.[4]

Second Schedule

List of documents to which the acknowledgement relates

4   Please refer to the Appendix pp 299ff for observations concerning rights to be excepted.

5

Conveyance of land comprising part of the garden of the vendor's house subject to existing covenants and creating new covenants[1]

This Conveyance dated
is made between:
(1) the Vendor
(2) the Purchaser

1 The Vendor acknowledges the receipt from the Purchaser of £   the purchase price of the land described in the first schedule ('the Property').

2 The Vendor as beneficial owner conveys to the Purchaser the fee simple estate in the Property.

3 The Property is subject to such covenants and restrictions contained in a conveyance dated *etc* as are still effective and relate to the Property.

4 The Purchaser covenants with the Vendor:

    (a) to perform and observe the covenants and restrictions referred to in clause 3 so far as they relate to the property and to indemnify the Vendor against any liability resulting from any future breach or non-observance;

    (b) to perform the covenants set out in the second schedule.

5 The Purchaser also covenants with the Vendor for the benefit of the whole and every part of the land shown edged blue on the attached plan[2] ('the Retained Premises') and so as to bind the whole and every part of the Property that he will observe the restrictive covenants set out in the third schedule [but the Purchaser shall be under no liability for any breach occurring after he has parted with all his interest in the Property].

6 The Vendor covenants with the Purchaser to indemnify the Purchaser against liability resulting from any breach or non-observance of the covenants referred to in clause 3 so far as they relate to the Retained Premises.

7 The parties declare that no rights over the Retained Premises shall vest in the Purchaser by implication as a result of both the Property and the Retained Premises being owned by the Vendor prior to the execution of this deed.[3]

8 The Vendor undertakes to keep safe the documents listed in the fourth schedule and acknowledges the right of the Purchaser to their production and to the supply of copies.

1   This precedent can easily be adapted to the sale of part of a plot of land. Please refer to the Appendix (pp 299ff) for observations of general application to sales-off.

2   Usually a plan will be required to define the land being sold in which case it is desirable to show the retained premises on the same plan rather than to describe it as 'the remainder of the land comprised in a conveyance dated *etc*'.
The covenants would almost certainly enure to the benefit of every part of the land without an addition of the words, 'of the whole and every part of': see *Federated Homes Ltd v Mill Lodge Properties Ltd* [1980] 1 All ER 371, but it was held in *Roake v Chadha* [1983] 3 All ER 503 that there may be exceptional cases that depend on the construction of the covenant as a whole.

3   Unless the doctrine in *Wheeldon v Burrows* is excluded, quasi easements etc enjoyed by the Property over the Retained Premises while they were in the ownership of the Vendor will pass to the Purchaser. This could result in the Purchaser acquiring, for example, a right of way over the Retained Premises contrary to the Vendor's expectation. Please refer to the Appendix (pp 299ff) for a more comprehensive statement concerning implied grants.

Add any appropriate standard clauses

Certificate of value (if applicable)

First Schedule
The land shown edged red on the attached plan
The following rights are included in this Conveyance:
Set out easements etc to be granted[4]
The following rights are excepted from this Coveyance:
Set out rights to be excepted[4]

Second Schedule
Set out positive covenants[5]

Third Schedule
Set out restrictive covenants[6]

Fourth Schedule
List documents to which the acknowledgement relates

4   It is very important that rights granted and excepted are carefully defined particularly any rights of way, rights to tie into existing sewers and to use other existing conduits. The draftsman should give careful thought to what rights will be required by both the Vendor and the Purchaser. See Appendix (p 299).

5   It is almost certain that there will be positive covenants such as to fence and to build in accordance with approved plans.

6   The Vendor may wish to impose restrictive covenants additional to those referred to in clause 3. Consideration must also be given as to whether the Purchaser ought to seek to impose restrictive covenants on the Vendor in relation to the Retained Premises. It must be remembered that, while the Vendor may be bound by the restrictive covenants referred to in clause 3, the Purchaser himself will not be able to enforce those covenants. Consequently it may be desirable to substitute for clause 6 a clause along the following lines:

The Vendor covenants with the Purchaser for the benefit of the whole and every party of the Property and so as to bind the whole and every part of the Retained Premises that:

(a) he will perform and observe the covenants and restrictions referred to in clause 3 so far as they relate to the Retained Premises and will indemnify *etc*;

(b) he will observe the restrictive convenants set out in the   schedule.

6

Conveyance by way of gift

This Deed of Gift dated
is made between:
(1) The Donor
(2) the Beneficiary

1 The Donor by way of gift[1] conveys to the Beneficiary the fee simple estate in the land and house known as [*postal address*] which is fully described in a convenance dated *etc*.

Add any standard clauses[2]

It is certified that this instrument falls within category L in the Schedule to the Stamp Duty (Exempt Instruments) Regulations 1987.[3]

1   It is not usual for a donor to give covenants for title or other implied covenants although there is no reason why he should not convey 'as settlor' which only implies a covenant for further assurances.

2   Apart from any other standard clause, the donor will wish to be indemnified if restrictive covenants affect the property.

3   Provided that this certificate is included, the deed is exempt from stamp duty. It does not require to be adjudicated nor produced to the Stamp Office.

7

Conveyance by way of exchange without payment of equality money[1]

This Deed of Exchange dated
is made between:
(1) AB *etc* ('Mr B')
(2) CD *etc* ('Mr D')
who have agreed to exchange the properties specified in the first schedule
and the second schedule which are of equal value.

1   Mr B as beneficial owner conveys to Mr D the fee simple estate in
the land described in the first schedule.

2   Mr D as beneficial owner conveys to Mr B the fee simple estate in
the land described in the second schedule.

Add any appropriate standard clauses[2]

First Schedule
Description of land conveyed by Mr B to Mr D

Second Schedule
Description of land conveyed by Mr D to Mr B

1   Precedent 9 can be adapted if its format is preferred or it is thought to be better suited to the transaction.

2   No certificate of value is required because ad valorem stamp duty is not attracted. The deed requires to be stamped 50p. See note 1 to next precedent relating to stamp duty on deeds of exchange generally.

8

Conveyance by way of exchange with payment of equality money

This Deed of Exchange dated
is made between:
(1) AB *etc* ('Mr B')
(2) CD *etc* ('Mr D')

1 Mr B acknowledges the receipt from Mr D of £ constituting the agreed difference between the value of the property described in the first schedule and the value of the property described in the second schedule.

2 Mr B as beneficial owner conveys to Mr D the fee simple estate in the land described in the first schedule.

3 Mr D as beneficial owner conveys to Mr B the fee simple estate in the land described in the second schedule.

Add any appropriate standard clauses

Certificate of value (if applicable) [1]

First Schedule
Description of land conveyed by Mr B to Mr D

Second Schedule
Description of land conveyed by Mr D to Mr B

1   Ad valorem stamp duty is payable on the amount paid as equality of exchange.
The following is a summary of the stamp duty requirements relating to exchanges:
(A) If there is a payment of equality money and
    (i) the payment exceeds the stamp duty threshold—ad valorem duty;
    (ii) the payment does not exceed the stamp duty threshold—certificate of value and
      no duty payable if the exchange is freehold for freehold, otherwise certificate for
      value and duty of 50p payable;
(B) If there is no payment of equality money—no certificate of value and duty of 50p
    payable.

9

Conveyance by way of exchange with payment of equality money—alternative form where one of the properties is subject to restrictive covenants

This Deed of Exchange dated
is made between:
(1) AB and LB *etc* ('Mr and Mrs B');
(2) CD and MD *etc* ('Mr and Mrs D')

1 (a) Mr and Mrs B are the owners of the land and house known as [10 Mercers Road *etc*] ('10 Mercers Road') which is fully described in a conveyance dated *etc* ('the 1972 Conveyance');

   (b) Mr and Mrs D are the owners of the land and house known as [378 Rochdale Road *etc*] ('378 Rochdale Road') which is fully described in a conveyance dated *etc* ('the 1960 Conveyance').

2 Mr and Mrs B acknowledge the receipt from Mr and Mrs D of £   constituting the agreed difference between the value of 10 Mercers Road and the value of 378 Rochdale Road.[1]

3 Mr and Mrs B as trustees[2] convey to Mr and Mrs D the fee simple estate in 10 Mercers Road.

4 Mr and Mrs D as trustees[2] convey to Mr and Mrs B the fee simple estate in 378 Rochdale Road.

5 10 Mercers Road is subject to such covenants and restrictions contained in [the 1972 Conveyance] as are still effective and Mr and Mrs D jointly and severally covenant with Mr and Mrs B to indemnify them against liability resulting from any future breach or non-observance of those covenants.

6 Mr and Mrs B declare that in equity they are joint tenants [*or as the case may be*].[3]

7 Mr and Mrs D declare that in equity they are joint tenants [*or as the case may be*].[3]

Add any other appropriate standard clauses

Certificate of value (if applicable)[4]

1   If this precedent is adapted for an exchange without the payment of equality money, substitute for this clause the following:
   The parties agree that 10 Mercers Road and 378 Rochdale Road are of equal value.
2   See Appendix (pp 299ff).

3   See Standard Clauses pp 292ff for other clauses relating to joint ownership.

4   See note 1 to preceding precedent.

10

Conveyance of property to which the Vendor has only a possessory title

This Conveyance dated
is made between:
(1) the Vendor
(2) the Purchaser

1 The Vendor acknowledges the receipt of £   the purchase price of the property described in the schedule ('the Property').

2 The Vendor as trustee[1] conveys to the Purchaser all his estate and interest in the Property.

3 The Vendor warrants[2] that:

(a) he has been in undisturbed and uninterrupted possession of the Property since [*date*] without acknowledging any other persons claim to ownership;

(b) he has not granted to any other person any interest or right in the Property.

Add any appropriate standard clauses

Certificate of value (if applicable)

Schedule

Description of the Property

1   The Vendor can only give a covenant for title in respect of his own acts and he should therefore convey as 'trustee'. His title is good only against inferior claims or claims barred under the Limitation Act.

2   This clause can be adapted to the circumstances. In its present form the warranty is restricted to the Vendor's period of possession. As the Vendor can be sued on the warranty, he may be unwilling to give a warranty extending to events outside his personal knowledge, for example, during a period when his predecessor was in possession. Provision should be made in the contract for any warranties to be given by the Vendor. The Purchaser will usually require a statutory declaration of the facts on which the possessory title is based. This will be supplied at the pre-contract stage and its contents will enable the purchaser's solicitor to draft a suitably worded warranty to be included in the conveyance. For example clause 3(a) might include a reference to there having been no claim adverse to the vendor's possessory title.

11

Conveyance of property to part of which Vendor has only a possessory title[1]

This Conveyance dated
is made between:
(1) the Vendor
(2) the Purchaser

1 The Vendor acknowledges the receipt of £   the purchase price of the property conveyed by this deed.

2 The Vendor as beneficial owner conveys to the Purchaser the fee simple estate in the land and house known as [*postal address*] which is [fully described in a conveyance dated *etc* and] shown edged red on the attached plan.

3 The Vendor as trustee[2] conveys to the Purchaser all his estate and interest in the land shown edged blue on the attached plan ('the blue land').

4 The Vendor warrants[3] that:

    (a) he has been in undisturbed and uninterrupted possession of the blue land since [*date*] without acknowledging any other persons claim to ownership;

    (b) he has not granted to any other person any interest or right in the blue land.

Add any appropriate standard clauses[4]

Certificate of value (if applicable)

1 It is not altogether unusual to find that a small area of land has been acquired as an accretion to, say, the garden of a house. This precedent is specifically designed for that situation.

2 The Vendor can only give a covenant for title in respect of his own acts and he should therefore convey as trustee. His title is good only against inferior claims or claims barred under the Limitation Act.

3 See note 2 to preceding precedent. Where the possessory title relates only to an addition to the garden or a small extension of the boundaries of the Property, the requirements of the Purchaser may be less exacting.

4 If any standard clauses relate to the Property described in clause 2, it will be convenient, in clause 2, to assign a definition to that Property such as 'the red land'.

12

Conveyance by way of sub-sale of the entirety of the property contracted to be bought

This Conveyance dated
is made between:
(1) the Vendor
(2) the sub-Vendor[1]
(3) the Purchaser

1 (a) The Vendor has agreed to sell to the sub-Vendor at the price of
£   the land and house known as [*postal address*] ('the
Property') which is fully described in a conveyance dated *etc*;

(b) The sub-Vendor has since agreed to resell the property to the
Purchaser at the price of £   .

2 The Vendor acknowledges the receipt of £   paid to him by
the Purchaser at the direction of the sub-Vendor and the sub-Vendor
acknowledges the receipt of £   being the balance of the total
purchase price of £   paid by the Purchaser.

3 The Vendor as beneficial owner[2] and at the direction of the sub-
Vendor (directing as beneficial owner[2]) conveys to the Purchaser the fee
simple estate in the Property.

Add any appropriate standard clauses

Certificate of value (if applicable) [3]

1   If the resale is at an increased price, equities will subsist in favour of the sub-Vendor and they will pass only under an instrument in writing (LPA 1925, s 53). The sub-Vendor must therefore be a party to and should execute the deed. In other cases, although not essential, it is desirable for the sub-Vendor to be a party as the Purchaser may wish to join him in any proceedings that may arise.

2   The capacity in which the Vendor conveys will be governed by the contract between the Vendor and the sub-Vendor and the capacity in which the sub-Vendor conveys by his contract with the Purchaser. The same covenants are implied by a person who directs as beneficial owner as by a person who conveys as beneficial owner. See LPA 1925, s 76(2).

3   The stamp duty is ad valorem on the amount of the total purchase price paid by the Purchaser, if this is equal to or exceeds the price agreed in the contract between the Vendor and the sub-Vendor. If the contract price is greater, the stamp duty requires to be adjudicated and both the contract and the conveyance should be submitted to the Adjudication Office. Prima facie, ad valorem duty is payable on the contract price but it is understood that the Adjudication Office will agree to ad valorem duty on the price paid by the Purchaser if it can be established that it is the true market value at the date of the conveyance. If, however, the contract price exceeds the price paid by the Purchaser but is below the stamp duty limit, the usual certificate of value can be included, no duty is payable and the deed need not be adjudicated.

13

Conveyance by way of sub-sale of part of the property contracted to be bought

This Conveyance dated
is made between:
(1) the Vendor
(2) the sub-Vendor[1]
(3) the Purchaser

1   (a) The Vendor has agreed to sell to the sub-Vendor (together with other property not dealt with in this deed) the land and house known as [*postal address*] ('the Property') which is fully described in a conveyance dated *etc.*[2]

   (b) The sub-Vendor has since agreed to resell the Property to the Purchaser at the price of £   to be paid to the Vendor in part satisfaction of the total sum due to him from the sub-Vendor.

2   The Vendor acknowledges the receipt and the sub-Vendor acknowledges the payment of £   paid to the Vendor by the Purchaser at the direction of the sub-Vendor.

3   The Vendor as beneficial owner[3] at the direction of the sub-Vendor (directing as beneficial owner[3]) conveys to the Purchaser the fee simple estate in the Property.

Add any appropriate standard clauses[4]

Certificate of value (if applicable)[5]

1   See note 1 to preceding precedent.

2   It is possible that the part disposed of by sub-sale will be a piece of land in which case this sub-clause will, of course, need adapting, for example, by defining as 'the Property' the land described in a schedule. It may also be necessary to except rights in favour of the residue of the property contracted to be bought, as in the case of a sale-off. See Appendix (pp 299ff).

3   See note 2 to preceding precedent.
4   An acknowledgment for production will almost certainly be required.
5   The liability for stamp duty is as follows:

> If the purchase price payable under the contract between the Vendor and the sub-Vendor ('the contract price') is below the stamp duty threshold no duty is payable on the conveyance of the residue of the land to the sub-Vendor and the usual certificate of value is included in that conveyance. Where the conveyance to the Purchaser is also below the stamp duty threshold the usual certificate of value is included in that conveyance as well.
>
> Where, however, the conveyance to the Purchaser is above the stamp duty threshold, ad valorem duty is payable on that conveyance and no duty on the conveyance of the residue to the sub-Vendor, for example (assuming a threshold of £30,000), if the contract price were £30,000 and the price paid by the Purchaser £32,000, ad valorem duty would be payable on the conveyance to the Purchaser. In such circumstances, it is unlikely that a conveyance by way of sub-sale would be used: there would be no advantage to any party. It would be better in all respects for the sub-Vendor to take a conveyance of the whole of the property and then convey part to the Purchaser. The conveyance to the sub-Vendor would contain a certificate of value and no duty would be payable and the conveyance to the Purchaser would attract ad valorem duty.
>
> If the contract price is above the stamp duty threshold, the *contract* between the Vendor and sub-Vendor should be stamped with ad valorem duty. A certificate of value is included in neither conveyance and, upon production of the stamped contract, each conveyance is stamped 'Duty paid'. Where, however, the price paid by the Purchaser exceeds the contract price, the conveyance to the Purchaser will attract ad valorem duty on the price paid by the Purchaser and the conveyance of the residue to the sub-Vendor will not attract duty. There is no advantage in using a sub-sale conveyance. The sub-Vendor will take a conveyance of the whole of the property and then convey part to the Purchaser. Neither deed will contain a certificate of value. Both contracts and both deeds should be submitted to the Adjudication Office.

14

Conveyance of residue of the property contracted to be purchased after sub-sale of part to sub-purchaser

This Conveyance dated
is made between;
(1) the Vendor
(2) the Purchaser

1 (a) The Vendor has agreed to sell to the Purchaser the land and house known as [*postal address*] ('the Property') which is fully described in a conveyance dated *etc* together with other property not dealt with in this deed ('the other land') at a total purchase price of £　　　　('the total purchase price');[1]

(b) At the direction of the Purchaser the other land has been conveyed to a third party and £　　　　(the purchase price due to the Purchaser in respect of the other land) has been paid to the Vendor in part satisfaction of the total purchase price.

2 The Vendor acknowledges the receipt from the Purchaser of £　　　　the balance of the total purchase price.

3 The Vendor as beneficial owner conveys to the Purchaser the fee simple estate in the Property.

Add any appropriate standard clauses

Certificate of value (if applicable) [2]

1   It may be necessary for 'the Property' to be described in a schedule where, for example, rights in its favour have been excepted from the conveyance of the 'other land'.

2   See note 5 to preceding precedent.

15

Conveyance of freehold reversion of a single lease— provision for merger or non-merger where the conveyance is to the owner of the leasehold

This Conveyance dated
is made between:
(1) the Vendor
(2) the Purchaser

1 The Vendor acknowledges the receipt from the Purchaser of £   the purchase price of the freehold reversion in the land and houses known as [*postal address*] ('the Property') which is fully described in a lease dated *etc* ('the Lease').

2 The Vendor as beneficial owner conveys to the Purchaser the fee simple estate in the Property subject to the Lease but with the benefit of the ground rent created by the Lease and of the covenants and restrictions contained in the Lease.

3 The Purchaser as the owner of the fee simple estate and of the leasehold estate in the Property declares that from the date of this deed the Lease shall no longer continue in force but shall be merged in the fee simple.[1]

or

3 The Purchaser declares that notwithstanding that he is now the owner of the fee simple estate and of the leasehold estate in the Property the Lease shall continue in force and shall not merge with the fee simple.[1]

Add any appropriate standard clauses

Certificate of value (if applicable)

1   The present rules as to merger are to be found in LPA 1925, s 185 which substitutes the equitable rules for the common law rules so that 'there is no merger by operation of law only of any estate the beneficial interest in which would not be deemed to be merged or extinguished in equity'.

It is not sufficient that the freehold and leasehold estates are in the same person; they must be vested in that person in the same capacity and without the intervention of any vested estate or incumbrance eg a mortgage of the leasehold estate. Note also Landlord & Tenant Act 1954, s 30(2).

In general, whether there is a merger depends upon the intention of the estate owner. It is desirable, therefore, that his intention should be declared in the deed.

Clause 3 will, of course, be omitted if the grantee is not the owner of the leasehold.

16

Conveyance of freehold reversion of several leases—provision for merger or non-merger where the conveyance is to the owner of the leaseholds

This Conveyance dated
is made between:
(1) the Vendor
(2) the Purchaser

1 The Vendor acknowledges the receipt from the Purchaser of £   the purchase price of the freehold reversion in the land and houses known as [*postal address*] ('the Property') which is fully described in a conveyance dated *etc.*[1]

2 The Vendor as beneficial owner conveys to the Purchaser the fee simple estate in the Property subject to the leases specified in the schedule ('the Leases') but together with the benefit of the ground rents created by the Leases and of the covenants and restrictions contained in the Leases.

3 The Purchaser as the owner of the fee simple estate and of the leasehold estates in the Property declares that from the date of this deed the Leases shall no longer continue in force but shall be merged in the fee simple.[2]

or

3 The Purchaser declares that notwithstanding that he is now the owner of the fee simple estate and of the leasehold estates in the Property the Leases shall continue in force and shall not merge with the fee simple.[2]

Add any appropriate standard clauses

Certificate of value (if applicable)

Schedule

Date of Lease	Property	Parties	Term	Rent

1   This description is suitable where the whole of the land comprised in an earlier conveyance has been demised by the Leases. In other cases it is probably better to describe 'the Property' as:

being the land demised by the leases specified in the schedule ('the Leases')

In clause 2 'the Leases' would then be substituted for 'the leases specified in the schedule ("the Leases")'.

2   The present rules as to merger are to be found in LPA 1925, s 185 which substitutes the equitable rules for the common law rules so that 'there is no merger by operation of law only of any estate the beneficial interest in which would not be deemed to be merged or extinguished in equity'.

It is not sufficient that the freehold and leasehold estates are in the same person; they must be vested in that person in the same capacity and without the intervention of any vested estate or incumbrance eg a mortgage of the leasehold estate. Note also Landlord & Tenant Act 1954, s 30(2).

In general, whether there is a merger depends upon the intention of the estate owner. It is desirable, therefore, that his intention should be declared in the deed.

Clause 3 will, of course, be omitted if the grantee is not the owner of the leaseholds.

B   Joint owners

17

Conveyance to two persons as beneficial joint tenants

This Conveyance dated
is made between:
(1) the Vendor
(2) the Purchasers

1 The Vendor acknowledges the receipt from the Purchasers of £   the purchase price of the land and house known as [*postal address*] ('the Property') which is fully described in a Conveyance dated *etc.*

2 The Vendor as beneficial owner conveys to the Purchasers the fee simple estate in the Property.

3 The Purchasers declare that they are beneficial joint tenants.[1]

Add any appropriate standard clauses

Certificates of value (if applicable)

1   Where, as in this case, the trustees are also the beneficial owners they have ample powers to deal with the Property either as trustees or as beneficial owners. It is not thought necessary, therefore, to give them, as trustees, additional powers to mortgage etc. The faint-hearted may, however, prefer to substitute the following for clause 3:

The Purchasers declare that:

(a) they are beneficial joint tenants;

(b) the trustees for sale of the Property shall have powers to deal with it equal to those of a sole beneficial owner.

18

Conveyance to two person as beneficial tenants in common

This Conveyance dated
is made between:
(1) the Vendor
(2) the Purchasers

1 The Vendor acknowledges the receipt from the Purchasers of
£ the purchase price of the land and house known as [*postal address*] ('the Property') which is fully described in a conveyance dated *etc.*

2 The Vendor as beneficial owner conveys to the Purchasers the fee simple estate in the Property.

3 The Purchasers declare that they are tenants in common in equal shares.

or

3 The Purchasers declare that they are tenants in common in the following shares: AB three-fifths and CD two-fifths.

or

3 The Purchasers declare that they are tenants in common in the proportions in which the purchase money was provided namely £ by AB and £ by CD

Add any appropriate standard clauses

Certificate of value (if applicable)

19

Conveyance by joint tenants

This Conveyance dated
is made between:
(1) the Vendors
(2) the Purchaser

1 The Vendors acknowledge the receipt from the Purchaser of
£   the purchase price of the land and house known as [*postal
address*] ('the Property') which is fully described in a conveyance dated
etc.

2 The Vendors as trustees[1] convey to the Purchaser the fee simple
estate in the Property.

Add any appropriate standard clauses

Certificate of value (if applicable)

1   Unless the contract provides otherwise, it is not thought that the Purchaser can require the Vendors to convey other than as trustees, although there does not appear to be any authority directly on this point. The capacity in which the Vendors convey is a matter of importance to the Purchaser because of the covenants implied by LPA 1925 s 76. Where the Property is leasehold or subject to rentcharge, it is an even more important matter because of the covenants implied by s 77. See Appendix (pp 299ff).

20

Conveyance by the survivor of joint owners, the vendor being solely and beneficially entitled[1]

This Conveyance dated
is made between:
(1) the Vendor
(2) the Purchaser

(A) Before [*date of death of deceased joint owner*] the Vendor and [*name of deceased joint owner*] were legally and beneficially entitled as joint tenants to the land and house known as [*postal address*] ('the Property') which is fully described in a conveyance dated *etc*.

(B) [*Name of deceased joint owner*] died on [*date*] and as a result the Vendor became solely and beneficially entitled to the Property.

1 The Vendor acknowledges the receipt from the Purchaser of £   the purchase price of the Property.

2 The Vendor as beneficial owner conveys to the Purchaser the fee simple estate in the Property.

Add any appropriate standard clause

Certificate of value (if applicable)

1   Law of Property (Joint Tenants) Act 1964, s 1 provides that, where property has been vested in two or more persons as joint tenants at law and in equity, the survivor of them shall, in favour of a purchaser of the legal estate, be deemed to be solely and beneficially interested if he conveys as beneficial owner or the conveyance includes a statement that he is so interested, unless a memorandum of severance has been endorsed on or attached to the conveyance to the joint tenants or any of them has become bankrupt. Clause (B) constitutes a statement that the survivor is solely and beneficially interested and, by clause 2, the Vendor conveys as beneficial owner. The precedent, therefore, doubly satisfies the provisions of the section.

21

Conveyance by surviving tenant in common with appointment of new trustee[1]

This Conveyance dated
is made between:
(1) the Vendors AB of *etc* and CD of *etc*
(2) the Purchaser

(A) By a conveyance dated *etc* ('the Conveyance') the fee simple estate in the land house known as [*postal address*] ('the Property') which is fully described in [the Conveyance] was vested in AB and EF as trustees for sale.

(B) EF died on [*date*].

1 AB appoints CD to be a trustee with him of the trust for sale created by the Conveyance.

2 The Vendors acknowledge the receipt from the Purchaser of £   the purchase price of the Property.

3 The Vendors as trustees convey to the Purchaser the fee simple estate in the Property.

Add any appropriate standard clauses

Certificate of value (if applicable)

1   This precedent is for use where it is intended from the outset that a new trustee should be appointed. The new trustee need not be a party to the contract but provision should be made in the contract for his appointment in the purchase deed. A separate deed of appointment should be used where land other than that being sold is also subject to the trust for sale.

22

Conveyance by one joint owner to the other[1]

This Conveyance dated
is made between:
(1) the Vendor
(2) the Purchaser

1 The Vendor acknowledges the receipt from the Purchaser of £ the purchase price of the Vendor's interest in the land and house known as [*postal address*] ('the Property') which is fully described in a conveyance dated *etc.*

2 The Vendor as beneficial owner conveys and releases to the Purchaser his interest in the Property.

3 The Vendor and the Purchaser as trustees[2] convey to the Purchaser the fee simple estate in the Property.

Add any appropriate standard clauses

Certificate of value (if applicable) [3]

1   Where A and B are joint tenants and A purchases B's share there are two methods by which the Property can be vested in A:
  (a) B can release his interest in the legal estate to A. See LPA 1925 s 36(2); or
  (b) A and B can convey the legal estate to A. See s 72(4).
This precedent employs a combination of these methods. The reason for this is that the provisions of s 36(2) are not altogether clear. The sub-section preserves the right of a joint tenant of the legal estate to release his interest to the other joint tenant. The word 'interest' normally connotes an *equitable* right. But the context may suggest that the sub-section refers to the joint tenant's share in the *legal* estate. If this is correct, it is argued that a subsequent purchaser ought to ensure that the equitable joint tenancy had not been severed prior to the release. The combination of a release and a conveyance of the legal estate avoids these problems because it matters not whether, at the time of the execution of the deed, the joint owners are, in equity, joint tenants or tenants in common.

2   It is appropriate that the Vendor should convey his equitable interest as beneficial owner but that he and the Purchaser should convey the legal estate as trustees.

3   The stamp duty is ad valorem on the purchase price for the vendor's interest.

23

Conveyance by owner to himself and another

This Conveyance dated
is made between:
(1) the Vendor
(2) the Purchaser

1 The Vendor acknowledges the receipt from the Purchaser of £ the purchase price of the interest vested in the Purchaser by this deed in the land and house known as [*postal address*] ('the Property') which is fully described in a conveyance dated *etc.*

2 The Vendor as beneficial owner conveys to himself and the Purchaser the fee simple estate in the Property.

3 The Vendor and the Purchaser declare that they are beneficial joint tenants.

or

3 The Vendor and the Purchaser declare that they are tenants in common [in equal shares] *or* [in the following shares: the Vendor four-fifths and the Purchaser one-fifth].

Add any appropriate standard clauses

No certificate of value

24

Sale of share by one joint owner to a stranger, the other joint owner and the stranger being made joint owners[1]

This Conveyance dated
is made between:
(1) the Vendor
(2) the Joint Owner
(3) the Purchaser

The fee simple estate in the land and house known as [*postal address*] ('the Property') which is fully described in a conveyance dated *etc* is vested in the Vendor and the Joint Owner.[2]

1 The Vendor acknowledges the receipt from the Purchaser of £   the purchase price of the Vendor's interest in the Property.

2 The Vendor as beneficial owner conveys his beneficial interest in the Property to the Purchaser.

3 The Vendor and the Joint Owner as trustees convey to the Joint Owner and the Purchaser the fee simple estate in the Property.

4 The Purchasers declare that they are tenants in common [in equal shares] *or* [in the following shares: the Joint Owner three-fifths and the Purchaser two-fifths].

Add any appropriate standard clauses

Certificate of value (if applicable)[3]

1 Consistent with the principles of the LPA 1925, some conveyancers will prefer to keep the assignment of the equitable interest off the title by having two deeds, one assigning the Vendor's beneficial interest and the other appointing the Purchaser as trustee of the legal estate in place of the Vendor.

2 If the Vendor and the Joint Owner are beneficial joint tenants, the sale by the Vendor will operate to sever the joint tenancy and a memorandum of severance should be endorsed on the conveyance creating the beneficial joint tenancy.

3 Stamp duty ad valorem on the purchase price paid by the purchaser to the vendor.

25

Conveyance to two persons jointly where the previous conveyance was to one of them although the purchase price had been provided jointly

This Conveyance dated
is made between:
(1) AB of *etc* ('Mr B');
(2) CD of *etc* ('Mr D').

(A) This conveyance is supplemental to a conveyance dated *etc* ('the Original Conveyance').

(B) By the Original Conveyance the fee simple estate in the land and house known as [*postal address*] ('the Property') was vested in Mr B.

(C) Mr D contributed to the purchase price paid for the property by Mr B and since the date of the Original Conveyance Mr B has held the Property as trustee for himself and Mr D.

(D) This deed is intended to regularise the position.

1 Mr B as trustee conveys to himself and Mr D the fee simple estate in the Property.

2 Mr B and Mr D declare that they are tenants in common [in equal shares] *or* [in the following shares: Mr B three-fifths and Mr C two-fifths].[1]

No standard clauses likely to be required as the deed is supplemental to the original conveyance

No certificate of value required[2]

1   Or '. . . beneficial joint tenants' if that be the case.

2   Stamp duty 50p.

26

Conveyance by Trustees for Sale

This Conveyance dated
is made between:
(1) the Vendors
(2) the Purchaser

1 The Vendors acknowledge the receipt from the Purchaser of
£   the purchase price of the land and house known as [*postal address*] ('the Property') which is fully described in a conveyance dated *etc.*

2 The Vendors as trustees convey to the Purchaser the fee simple estate in the Property.

Add any appropriate standard clauses

Certificate of value (if applicable)

27

Conveyance to partners

This Conveyance dated
is made between:
(1) the Vendor
(2) the Purchasers

1 The Vendor acknowledges the receipt from the Purchasers of £   the purchase price of the land and [building][1] known as [*postal address*] ('the Property') which is fully described in a conveyance dated *etc*.

2 The Vendor as beneficial owner conveys to the Purchasers the fee simple estate in the Property.

3 The Purchasers declare that they hold the Property as part of their partnership property and that the trustees for sale of the Property shall have powers to deal with it equal to those of a sole beneficial owner.[2]

Add any appropriate standard clauses

Certificate of value (if applicable)

1　It may be possible to give a more accurate description, such as office, factory or the like.

2　The Property will be held by the Purchasers on trust for sale and the fact that there is a reference to its being partnership property will not affect a Purchaser with notice of the trust. See LPA 1925, s 27(1). The provision that the partners shall hold the property as part of their partnership assets enables the partners subsequently to re-arrange their shares in the partnership without reference to the Property conveyed by this deed. In effect, the value of the partners' interests in the Property will be reflected by their capital accounts. If the precise share of the Property to be held by each partner is to be specified, it is better to convey the Property to the Purchasers as tenants in common, without reference to the partnership or to partnership property.

28

Conveyance to trustees of an existing trust

This Conveyance dated
is made between:
(1) the Vendor
(2) the Purchasers

1 The Vendor acknowledges the receipt from the Purchasers of £   the purchase price of the land and house known as [*postal address*] ('the Property') which is fully described in a conveyance dated *etc.*

2 The Vendor as beneficial owner conveys to the Purchasers the fee simple estate in the Property.

3 The Purchasers declare that they are trustees for sale and hold the Property on the trusts created by [*Will deed or other instrument which sets out the trust*] ('the Trust Deed').[1]

4 The power of appointing new trustees of the trust for sale created by this deed is vested in [the Purchasers].[2]

5 Under the terms of [*the trust deed*] the Purchasers have the following powers:
Set out additional powers granted by the trust deed

Add any appropriate standard clauses

Certificate of value (if applicable)

1   The reference to the trust deed will not affect a Purchaser with notice of the trust. See LPA 1925, s 27(1).

2   It is desirable that the provision in the trust deed for the appointment of new trustees is set out in this deed. Although a future purchaser from the trustees will not be affected by the trusts themselves, he will have to verify who are the trustees able to make title and it is undesirable that, for this purpose, resort should be had to the trust deed itself. Similarly any additional powers available to the trustees should be specifically mentioned in this deed.

C   Joint owners—husband and wife

29

Conveyance by husband to himself and his wife—no existing mortgage[1]

This Conveyance dated
is made between:
(1) A B of *etc* ('Mr B');
(2) his wife C B of the same address ('Mrs B').

1   By way of gift Mr B as beneficial owner[2] conveys to himself and Mrs B the fee simple estate in the land and house known as [*postal address*] which is fully described in a conveyance dated *etc*.

2   The same covenants shall be implied in this deed as if it had been for valuable consideration.

3   Mr B and Mrs B declare that they are beneficial joint tenants.

or

3   Mr B and Mrs B declare that they are tenants in common in equal shares [*or as the case may be*].

Add any appropriate standard clauses

4   It is certified that this instrument falls within category L in the Schedule to the Stamp Duty (Exempt Instruments) Regulations 1987.[3]

1   It is not uncommon for property, especially the matrimonial home, to have been vested in the husband's name at the time of its purchase and for the husband to wish to vest it in joint names some years later. This precedent is not, therefore, intended to apply to a transfer resulting from a dispute.

2   In the circumstances set out in note 1 above, the husband will usually wish to convey as beneficial owner but, as the conveyance is not for valuable consideration, clause 2 should be included to ensure that the full benefit of beneficial owner covenants are obtained.

3   Provided that this certificate is included the deed is exempt from stamp duty. It does not require to be adjudicated nor produced to the Stamp Office.

30

Conveyance by husband to himself and his wife—property subject to existing mortgage[1]

This Conveyance dated
is made between:
(1) AB of *etc* ('Mr B');
(2) his wife CB of the same address ('Mrs B');
(3) the   Building Society *etc* ('the Society').

Mr B is the owner of the land and house known as [*postal address*] ('the Property') which is fully described in a conveyance dated *etc* subject to a mortgage dated   and made between Mr B and the Society ('the Mortgage').

1   By way of gift and with the consent of the Society Mr B as beneficial owner[2] conveys to himself and Mrs B subject to the Mortgage the fee simple estate in the Property.

2   The same covenants shall be implied in this deed as if it had been for valuable consideration.

3   Mr B and Mrs B jointly and severally covenant with the Society to observe the provisions contained in the Mortgage as if they had both been the original borrowers.

4   Mr B and Mrs B declare that they are beneficial joint tenants [*or as the case may be*].

Add any appropriate standard clauses

5   It is certified that this instrument falls within category L in the Schedule to the Stamp Duty (Exempt Instruments) Regulations 1987.[3]

1   It is not uncommon for property, especially the matrimonial home, to have been vested in the husband's name at the time of its purchase and for the husband to wish to vest it in joint names some years later. This precedent is not, therefore, intended to apply to a transfer resulting from a dispute. It is not essential that the mortgagee should join in the conveyance (unless there is a prohibition in the mortgage against transfer without consent) but it is desirable, in the circumstances of this transaction, that the mortgagee should consent to the transfer. There is little point in the building society releasing the husband from his covenant to pay. If the mortgagee is not joined in the conveyance, precedent 97 should be adapted to the circumstances of the transaction.

2   In the circumstances set out in note 1 above, the husband will usually wish to convey as beneficial owner but, as the conveyance is not for valuable consideration, clause 2 should be included to ensure that the full benefit of beneficial owner covenants are obtained.

3   Provided that this certificate is included the deed is exempt from stamp duty. It does not require to be adjudicated nor produced to the Stamp Office.

31

Conveyance in settlement of a matrimonial dispute by husband to his wife of property not subject to a mortgage—no payment made by wife to husband

This Conveyance dated
is made between:

(1) AB of *etc* ('Mr B');

(2) his [former] wife CB of *etc* ('Mrs B').

1 This conveyance gives effect to the settlement between the parties of a matrimonial dispute.[1]

2 Mr B as beneficial owner[2] conveys to Mrs B the fee simple estate in the land and house known as [*postal address*] which is fully described in a conveyance dated *etc*.

3 The same covenants shall be implied in this deed as if it had been for valuable consideration.

Add any appropriate standard clauses

4 It is certified that this instrument falls within category H in the Schedule to the Stamp Duty (Exempt Instruments) Regulations 1987.[3]

1   If the conveyance is executed pursuant to a court order, the following should be substituted for clause 1:

> This conveyance is made in compliance with an Order of the   County Court dated   in proceedings between Mrs B and Mr B [*or as the case may be*] under case number   .

2   It is thought that Mr B should convey as beneficial owner. The terms of the settlement or the court order will constitute consideration for Mr B's executing the conveyance and Mrs B ought, therefore, to have the benefit of the covenants implied in the conveyance as a result of Mr B conveying as beneficial owner. In this event, clause 3 should be included in order to obtain the full benefit of beneficial owner covenants.

3   Provided that this certificate is included the deed is exempt from stamp duty. It does not require to be adjudicated nor produced to the Stamp Office. It does not matter whether there is a court order or not. Category H covers conveyances made pursuant to a court order in matrimonial proceedings and conveyances 'in pursuance of an agreement of the parties made in contemplation of or otherwise in connection with' matrimonial proceedings.

32

Conveyance in settlement of a matrimonial dispute by husband to his wife of property not subject to a mortgage— payment made by wife to husband

This Conveyance dated
is made between:
(1) AB of *etc* ('Mr B');
(2) his [former] wife CB of *etc* ('Mrs B').

1   This conveyance gives effect to the settlement between the parties of a matrimonial dispute.[1]

2   Mr B acknowledges the receipt from Mrs B of £   .[2]

3   Mr B as beneficial owner[3] conveys to Mrs B the fee simple estate in the land and house known as [*postal address*] which is fully described in conveyance dated *etc*.

Add any appropriate standard clauses

4   It is certified that this instrument falls within category H in the Schedule to the Stamp Duty (Exempt Instruments) Regulations 1987.[4]

1   If the conveyance is executed pursuant to a court order, the following should be substituted for clause 1:

This conveyance is made in compliance with an order of the   County Court dated   in proceedings between Mrs B and Mr B [*or as the case may be*] under case number   .

2   The payment is not described as the purchase price because it may not represent the value of the interest transferred but a negotiated payment taking account of a variety of considerations.

3   It is thought that Mr B should convey as beneficial owner. The terms of the settlement or the court order will constitute consideration for Mr B's executing the conveyance and Mrs B ought, therefore, to have the benefit of the covenants implied in the conveyance as a result of Mr B's conveying as beneficial owner.

4   Provided that this certificate is included the deed is exempt from stamp duty. It does not require to be adjudicated nor produced to the Stamp Office. It does not matter whether there is a court order or not. Category H covers conveyances made pursuant to a court order in matrimonial proceedings and conveyances 'in pursuance of an agreement of the parties made in contemplation of or otherwise in connection with' matrimonial proceedings.

33

Conveyance in settlement of a matrimonial dispute by husband to his wife of property subject to a mortgage—mortgagee joining in conveyance—no payment made by wife to husband

This Conveyance dated
is made between:
(1) AB of *etc* ('Mr B');
(2) his [former] wife CB of *etc* ('Mrs B');
(3)   Building Society of *etc* ('the Society').

Mr B is the owner of the land and house known as [*postal address*] ('the Property') which is fully described in a conveyance dated *etc* subject to a mortgage dated   and made between (1) Mr B and (2) the Society ('the Mortgage').

1 This conveyance gives effect to the settlement between Mr B and Mrs B of a matrimonial dispute.[1]

2 Mr B as beneficial owner[2] conveys to Mrs B subject to the Mortgage the fee simple estate in the Property.

3 The same covenants shall be implied in this deed as if it had been for valuable consideration.

4 The Society consents to the transfer of the Property to Mrs B and from the date of this deed releases Mr B from his obligations under the Mortgage other than his covenants for title.

5 Mrs B covenants with the Society that she will from the date of this deed observe the provisions of the Mortgage as if she alone had been the original borrower.

Add any appropriate standard clauses

6 It is certified that this instrument falls within category H in the Schedule to the Stamp Duty (Exempt Instruments) Regulations 1987.[3]

1   If the conveyance is executed pursuant to a court order, the following should be substituted for clause 1:

This conveyance is made in compliance with an order of the   County Court dated   in proceedings between Mrs B and Mr B [*or as the case may be*] under case number   .

2   It is thought that Mr B should convey as beneficial owner. The terms of the settlement or the court order will constitute consideration for Mr B's executing the conveyance and Mrs B ought, therefore, to have the benefit of the covenants implied in the conveyance as a result of Mr B's conveying as beneficial owner. In this event clause 3 should be included in order to obtain the full benefit of beneficial owner covenants.

3   Provided that this certificate is included the deed is exempt from stamp duty. It does not require to be adjudicated nor produced to the Stamp Office. It does not matter whether there is a court order or not. Category H covers conveyances made pursuant to a court order in matrimonial proceedings and conveyances 'in pursuance of an agreement of the parties made in contemplation of or otherwise in connection with' matrimonial proceedings.

34

Conveyance in settlement of a matrimonial dispute by husband to his wife of property subject to a mortgage—mortgagee joining in conveyance—payment made by wife to husband

This Conveyance dated
is made between:
(1) AB of *etc* ('Mr B');
(2) his [former] wife CB of *etc* ('Mrs B');
(3)   Building Society of *etc* ('the Society').
Mr B and Mrs B are the beneficial joint owners of the land and house known as [*postal address*] ('the Property') which is fully described in a conveyance dated *etc* subject to a mortgage dated   and made between (1) Mr B and Mrs B and (2) the Society ('the Mortgage').

1 This conveyance gives effect to the settlement between Mr B and Mrs B of a matrimonial dispute.[1]

2 Mr B acknowledges the receipt from Mrs B of £   .[2]

3 Mr B as beneficial owner[3] conveys to Mrs B subject to the Mortgage the fee simple estate in the Property.

4 The Society consents to the transfer of the property to Mrs B and from the date of this deed releases Mr B from his obligations under the Mortgage.

5 Mrs B covenants with the Society that she will from the date of this deed observe the provisions of the Mortgage as if she alone had been the original borrower.

Add any appropriate standard clauses

6 It is certified that this instrument falls within category H in the Schedule to the Stamp Duty (Exempt Instruments) Regulations 1987.[4]

1   If the conveyance is executed pursuant to a court order, the following should be substituted for clause 1:

This conveyance is made in compliance with an order of the   County Court dated   in proceedings between Mr B and Mrs B [*or as the case may be*] under case number   .

2   The payment is not described as the purchase price because it may not represent the value of the interest transferred but a negotiated payment taking account of a variety of considerations.

3   It is thought that Mr B should convey as beneficial owner. The terms of the settlement or the court order will constitute consideration for Mr B's executing the conveyance and Mrs B ought, therefore, to have the benefit of the covenants implied in the conveyance as a result of Mr B's conveying as beneficial owner.

4   Provided that this certificate is included the deed is exempt from stamp duty. It does not require to be adjudicated nor produced to the Stamp Office. It does not matter whether there is a court order or not. Category L covers conveyances made pursuant to a court order in matrimonial proceedings and conveyances 'in pursuance of an agreement of the parties made in contemplation of or otherwise in connection with' matrimonial proceedings.

35

Conveyance in settlement of a matrimonial dispute by husband as one joint owner to his wife as the other of property not subject to a mortgage—no payment made by wife to husband

This Conveyance dated
is made between:
(1) AB of *etc* ('Mr B');
(2) his [former] wife CB of *etc* ('Mrs B').

Mr B and Mrs B are the beneficial joint owners of the land and house known as [*postal address*] ('the Property') which is fully described in a conveyance dated *etc*.

1   This conveyance gives effect to the settlement between the parties of a matrimonial dispute.[1]

2   Mr B as beneficial owner[2] conveys and releases to Mrs B his interest in the Property.

3   Mr B and Mrs B as trustees[3] convey to Mrs B the fee simple estate in the Property.

4   The same covenants shall be implied in this deed as if it had been for valuable consideration.

Add any appropriate standard clauses

5   It is certified that this instrument falls within category H in the Schedule to the Stamp Duty (Exempt Instruments) Regulations 1987.[4]

1   If the conveyance is executed pursuant to a court order, the following should be substituted for clause 1:
> This conveyance is made in compliance with an order of the   County
> Court dated   in proceedings between Mr B and Mrs B [*or as the case may be*] under case number   .

2   It is thought that Mr B should convey as beneficial owner. The terms of the settlement or the court order will constitute consideration for Mr B's executing the conveyance and Mrs B ought, therefore, to have the benefit of the covenants implied in the conveyance as a result of Mr B's conveying as beneficial owner.

3   The argument that Mr and Mrs B should convey the legal estate as beneficial owners is not perhaps as strong as that in favour of Mr B's conveying his beneficial interest as beneficial owner. Nevertheless, many draftsmen will prefer to substitute 'as beneficial owners' for 'as trustees' in this clause.

4   Provided that this certificate is included the deed is exempt from stamp duty. It does not require to be adjudicated nor produced to the Stamp Office. It does not matter whether there is a court order or not. Category H covers conveyances made pursuant to a court order in matrimonial proceedings and conveyances 'in pursuance of an agreement of the parties made in contemplation of or otherwise in connection with' matrimonial proceedings.

36

Conveyance in settlement of a matrimonial dispute by husband as one joint owner to his wife as the other of property not subject to a mortgage—payment made by wife to husband

This Conveyance dated
is made between:
(1) AB of *etc* ('Mr B');
(2) his [former] wife CB of *etc* ('Mrs B').

Mr B and Mrs B are the beneficial joint owners of the land and house known as [*postal address*] ('the Property') which is fully described in a conveyance dated *etc*.

1 This conveyance gives effect to the settlement between the parties of a matrimonial dispute.[1]

2 Mr B acknowledges the receipt from Mrs B of £   .[2]

3 Mr B as beneficial owner[3] conveys and releases to Mrs B his interest in the Property.

4 Mr B and Mrs B as trustees[4] convey to Mrs B the fee simple estate in the Property.

Add any appropriate standard clauses

5 It is certified that this instrument falls within category H in the Schedule to the Stamp Duty (Exempt Instruments) Regulations 1987.[5]

1   If the conveyance is executed pursuant to a court order, the following should be substituted for clause 1 :

This conveyance is made in compliance with an order of the   County Court dated   in proceedings between Mrs B and Mr B [*or as the case may be*] under case number   .

2   The payment is not described as the purchase price because it may not represent the value of the interest transferred but a negotiated payment taking account of a variety of considerations.

3   It is thought that Mr B should convey as beneficial owner. The terms of the settlement or the court order will constitute consideration for Mr B's executing the conveyance and Mrs B ought, therefore, to have the benefit of the covenants implied in the conveyance as a result of Mr B's conveying as beneficial owner.

4   The argument that Mr and Mrs B should convey the legal estate as beneficial owners is not perhaps as strong as that in favour of Mr B's conveying his beneficial interest as beneficial owner. Nevertheless many draftsmen will prefer to substitute 'as beneficial owners' for 'as trustees' in this clause.

5   Provided that this certificate is included the deed is exempt from stamp duty. It does not require to be adjudicated nor produced to the Stamp Office. It does not matter whether there is a court order or not. Category H covers conveyances made pursuant to a court order in matrimonial proceedings and conveyances 'in pursuance of an agreement of the parties made in contemplation of or otherwise in connection with' matrimonial proceedings.

37

Conveyance in settlement of a matrimonial dispute by husband as one joint owner to his wife as the other of property subject to a mortgage—mortgagee joining in conveyance—no payment made by wife to husband

This Conveyance dated
is made between:

(1) AB of *etc* ('Mr B');
(2) his [former] wife CB of *etc* ('Mrs B');
(3)   Building Society of *etc* ('the Society').

Mr B and Mrs B are the beneficial joint owners of the land and house known as [*postal address*] ('the Property') which is fully described in a conveyance dated *etc* subject to a mortgage dated   and made between (1) Mr B and Mrs B and (2) the Society ('the Mortgage').

1   This conveyance gives effect to the settlement between Mr B and Mrs B of a matrimonial dispute.[1]

2   Mr B as beneficial owner[2] conveys and releases to Mrs B his interest in the Property.

3   Mr B and Mrs B as trustees[3] convey to Mrs B subject to the Mortgage the fee simple estate in the Property.

4   The same covenants shall be implied in this deed as if it had been for valuable consideration.

5   The Society consents to the transfer of the Property to Mrs B and from the date of this deed releases Mr B from his obligations under the Mortgage other than his covenants for title.

6   Mrs B covenants with the Society that she will from the date of this deed observe the provisions of the Mortgage as if she alone had been the original borrower.

Add any appropriate standard clauses

7   It is certified that this instrument falls within category H in the Schedule to the Stamp Duty (Exempt Instruments) Regulations 1987.[4]

1   If the conveyance is executed pursuant to a court order, the following should be substituted for clause 1:

This conveyance is made in compliance with an Order of the   County
Court dated   in proceedings between Mrs B and Mr B [*or as the case may be*] under case number   .

2   It is thought that Mr B should convey as beneficial owner. The terms of the settlement or the court order will constitute consideration for Mr B's executing the conveyance and Mrs B ought, therefore, to have the benefit of the covenants implied in the conveyance as a result of Mr B's conveying as beneficial owner.

3   The argument that Mr and Mrs B should convey the legal estate as beneficial owners is not perhaps as strong as that in favour of Mr B's conveying his beneficial interest as beneficial owner. Nevertheless, many draftsmen will prefer to substitute 'as beneficial owners' for 'as trustees' in this clause.

4   Provided that this certificate is included the deed is exempt from stamp duty. It does not require to be adjudicated nor produced to the Stamp Office. It does not matter whether there is a court order or not. Category H covers conveyances made pursuant to a court order in matrimonial proceedings and conveyances 'in pursuance of an agreement of the parties made in contemplation of or otherwise in connection with' matrimonial proceedings.

38

Conveyance in settlement of a matrimonial dispute by husband as one joint owner to his wife as the other of property subject to a mortgage—mortgagee joining in conveyance—payment made by wife to husband[1]

This Conveyance dated
is made between:

(1) AB of *etc* ('Mr B');

(2) his [former] wife CB of *etc* ('Mrs B');

(3) Building Society of *etc* ('the Society').

Mr B and Mrs B are the beneficial joint owners of the land and house known as [*postal address*] ('the Property') which is fully described in a conveyance dated *etc* subject to a mortgage dated and made between (1) Mr B and Mrs B and (2) the Society ('the Mortgage').

1 This conveyance gives effect to the settlement between Mr B and Mrs B of a matrimonial dispute.[2]

2 Mr B acknowledges the receipt from Mrs B of £ .[3]

3 Mr B as beneficial owner[4] conveys and releases to Mrs B his interest in the Property.

3 Mr B and Mrs B as trustees[5] convey to Mrs B subject to the Mortgage the fee simple estate in the Property.

4 The Society consents to the transfer of the Property to Mrs B and from the date of this deed releases Mr B from his obligations under the Mortgage other his covenants for title.

5 Mrs B covenants with the Society that she will from the date of this deed observe the provisions of the Mortgage as if she alone had been the original borrower.

Add any appropriate standard clauses

6 It is certified that this instrument falls within category H in the Schedule to the Stamp Duty (Exempt Instruments) Regulations 1987.[6]

1   This conveyance may sometimes be required but in many cases in which the property is subject to a mortgage and the wife makes a payment to the husband, it is necessary to obtain an increased mortgage to enable the payment to be made. In these circumstances precedent 32 would be used, the existing mortgage by the husband would be paid off and the wife would be the sole borrower under the new mortgage.

2   If the conveyance is executed pursuant to a court order, the following should be substituted for clause 1:
This conveyance is made in compliance with an order of the   County Court dated   in proceedings between Mrs B and Mr B [*or as the case may be*] under case number   .

3   The payment is not described as the purchase price because it may not represent the value of the interest transferred but a negotiated payment taking account of a variety of considerations.

4   It is thought that Mr B should convey as beneficial owner. The terms of the settlement or the court order will constitute consideration for Mr B's executing the conveyance and Mrs B ought, therefore, to have the benefit of the covenants implied in the conveyance as a result of Mr B's conveying as beneficial owner.

5   The argument that Mr & Mrs B should convey the legal estate as beneficial owners is not perhaps as strong as that in favour of Mr B's conveying his beneficial interest as beneficial owner. Nevertheless, many draftsmen will prefer to substitute 'as beneficial owners' for 'as trustees' in this clause.

6   Provided that this certificate is included the deed is exempt from stamp duty. It does not require to be adjudicated nor produced to the Stamp Office. It does not matter whether there is a court order or not. Category H covers conveyances made pursuant to a court order in matrimonial proceedings and conveyances 'in pursuance of an agreement of the parties made in contemplation of or otherwise in connection with' matrimonial proceedings.

D Personal representatives, trustees for sale, tenants for life and and statutory owners

39

Conveyance by personal representatives

This Conveyance dated
is made between:
(1) the Vendors
(2) the Purchaser

(A) At his death on   [*name of the deceased*] ('the deceased')
was the owner of the land and house known as [*postal address*] ('the
Property') which is fully described in a conveyance dated *etc*.

(B) On   the [Principal] *or* [District] Probate
Registry granted to the Vendors [Probate of the Will] *or* [Letters of
Administration of the estate] of the deceased ('the Grant').

(C) The Vendors have not previously made any assent or conveyance
affecting a legal estate in the Property.[1]

1   The Vendors acknowledge the receipt from the Purchaser of
£   the purchase price of the Property.

2   The Vendors as personal representatives convey to the Purchaser the
fee simple estate in the Property.

3   The Vendors acknowledge the right of the Purchaser to the production
of the Grant and to the supply of copies.[2]

Add any appropriate standard clauses

Certificate of value (if applicable)

1   See Administration of Estates Act 1925, s 36(6) for the effect of this statement. A memorandum of this conveyance should be endorsed on the grant.

2   An acknowledgment for the production of the grant will always be required but, of course, other deeds may have to be included as well. In this event, a schedule should be used. See standard clauses, pp 292ff.

40

Conveyance by a surviving personal representative

This Conveyance dated
is made between:
(1) the Vendor
(2) the Purchaser

(A) At his death on   [*name of deceased*] ('the deceased') was
the owner of the land and house known as [*postal address*] ('the Property')
which is fully described in a conveyance dated *etc*.

(B) On   the [Principal] *or* [District] Probate
Registry granted to the Vendor and AB [Probate of the Will] *or* [Letters
of Administration of the estate] of the deceased ('the Grant').

(C) AB died on [*date*].

(D) The Vendor has not either solely or jointly with AB previously made
any assent or conveyance affecting a legal estate in the Property .[1]

1 The Vendor acknowledges the receipt from the Purchaser of
£   the purchase price of the Property.

2 The Vendor as personal representative conveys to the Purchaser the
fee simple estate in the Property.

3 The Vendor acknowledges the right of the Purchaser to production
of the Grant and to the supply of copies.[2]

Add any appropriate standard clauses

Certificate of value (if applicable)

1 See Administration of Estates Act 1925, s 36(6) for the effect of this statement. A memorandum of this conveyance should be endorsed on the grant.

2 An acknowledgment for the production of the grant will always be required but, of course, other deeds may have to be included as well. In this event, a schedule should be used. See standard clauses, pp 292ff.

41

Conveyance by personal representative of a surviving beneficial joint tenant[1]

This Conveyance dated
is made between:
(1) the Vendor
(2) the Purchaser

(A) By a conveyance dated *etc* ('the Conveyance') the land and the house known as [*postal address*] ('the Property') which is fully described in the Conveyance was vested in AB and CD as beneficial joint tenants.

(B) AB died on [*date*] and CD then became the sole beneficial owner of the Property.

(C) CD died on [*date*].

(D) On   the [Principal] *or* [District] Probate Registry granted to the Vendor [Probate of the Will] *or* [Letters of Administration of the estate] of CD ('the Grant').

(E) The Vendor has not previously made any assent or conveyance affecting a legal estate in the Property.[2]

1 The Vendor acknowledges the receipt from the Purchaser of £   the purchase price of the Property.

2 The Vendor as personal representative conveys to the Purchaser the fee simple estate in the Property.

3 The Vendor acknowledges the right of the Purchaser to the production of the Grant and to the supply of copies.[3]

Add any appropriate standard clauses

Certificate of value (if applicable)

1   Law of Property (Joint Tenants) Act 1964, s 1 provides that, where property has been vested in two or more persons in law and in equity, the survivor of them shall, in favour of the purchaser of the legal estate, be deemed to be solely and beneficially entitled if he conveys as beneficial owner or the conveyance includes a statement that he is so interested, unless a memorandum of severance has been endorsed on or attached to the conveyance to the joint tenants or any of them has become bankrupt.

This provision applies 'with the necessary modifications' in relation to a conveyance by the personal representative of the survivor of joint tenants. Clause (B) constitutes a statement that the surviving joint tenant was solely and beneficially interested.

Where the original joint owners were beneficial tenants in common or the equitable joint tenancy has been severed, the next precedent should be used.

2   See Administration of Estates Act 1925, s 36(6) for the effect of this statement. A memorandum of this conveyance should be endorsed on the grant.

3   An acknowledgment for the production of the grant will always be required but, of course, other deeds may have to be included as well. In this event, a schedule should be used. See standard clauses, pp 292ff.

42

Conveyance by personal representatives of a surviving beneficial tenant in common[1]

This Conveyance dated
is made between:
(1) the Vendors
(2) the Purchaser

(A) By a conveyance dated *etc* ('the Conveyance') the land and house known as [*postal address*] ('the Property') which is fully described in the Conveyance was vested in AB and CD as beneficial tenants in common.

(B) AB died on [*date*] and CD died on [*date*].

(C) On   the [Principal] *or* [District] Probate Registry granted to the Vendors [Probate of the Will] *or* [Letters of Administration of the estate] of CD ('the Grant').

1   The Vendors acknowledge the receipt from the Purchaser of £   the purchase price of the Property.

2   The Vendors as trustees convey to the Purchaser the fee simple estate in the Property.

3   The Vendors acknowledge the right of the Purchaser to the production of the Grant and to the supply of copies.[2]

Add any appropriate standard clauses

Certificate of value (if applicable)

1   Trustee Act 1925, s 18 enables a personal representative of a sole trustee or of the survivor of trustees, pending the appointment of new trustees, to exercise any trust power which could have been exercised by the trustees subject to the restriction imposed by s 14 that a sole trustee cannot give a valid receipt for capital moneys. LPA 1925, s 27(2) enables a sole personal representative *as such* to give a valid receipt for capital money. It is thought, however, that the executor or administrator of a surviving beneficial tenant in common who sells the property is not acting as personal representative but as trustee and that he must appoint a co-trustee to give a valid receipt for the purchase price. This problem does not arise where there is more than one personal representative but if there is only one personal representative, a co-trustee must be appointed. See next precedent. Because the vendors sell as 'acting trustees' under Trustee Act 1925, s 18, and not as personal representatives, no declaration that there has been no previous assent or conveyance is required.

2   An acknowledgment for the production of the grant will always be required but, of course, other deeds may have to be included as well. In this event, a schedule should be used. See standard clauses, pp 292ff.

43

Conveyance by a sole representative of a surviving beneficial tenant in common with appointment of new trustee[1]

This Conveyance date
is made between:
(1) the Vendors MN of *etc* and OP of *etc*
(2) the Purchaser

(A) By a conveyance dated *etc* ('the Conveyance') the land and house known as [*postal address*] ('the Property') which is fully described in the Conveyance was vested in AB and CD as beneficial tenants in common.

(B) AB died on [*date*] and CD died on [*date*].

(C) On   the [Principal] *or* [District] Probate Registry granted to MN [Probate of the Will] *or* [Letters of Administration of the estate] of CD ('the Grant').

1 MN appoints himself and OP to be trustees of the trust for sale created by the Conveyance.[2]

2 The Vendors acknowledge the receipt from the Purchaser of £   the purchase price of the Property.

3 The Vendors as trustees convey to the Purchaser the fee simple estate in the Property.

4 MN acknowledges the right of the Purchaser to the production of the Grant and to the supply of copies.

Add any appropriate standard clauses

Certificate of value (if applicable)

1   See note 1 to preceding precedent.

2   It should be noted that the powers granted to a personal representative under s 18 are 'until the appointment of new trustees'. It is thought, therefore, that the personal representative should appoint both himself and OP as trustees and not merely appoint OP because the very appointment of OP would deprive the personal representative of his powers under s 18 and would leave OP a sole trustee unable to give a valid receipt for capital money.

44

Conveyance by tenant for life under Settled Land Act 1925[1]

This Conveyance
is made between:
(1) the Vendor
(2) the Trustees
(3) the Purchaser

The land and house known as [*postal address*] ('the Property') which is fully described in a conveyance dated *etc*[2] is vested in the Vendor as tenant for life under the Settled Land Act 1925 by a vesting deed dated *etc* and the Trustees are the trustees of the settlement for the purposes of that Act.

1 The Trustees acknowledge the receipt of £   the purchase price of the Property paid to them by the Purchaser at the direction of the Vendor.

2 The Vendor as trustee conveys to the Purchaser the fee simple estate in the Property.

Add any appropriate standard clauses

Certificate of value (if applicable)

1   Proof that the trustees are the existing trustees under SLA 1925 will be essential if the purchaser is to obtain the legal estate free from equitable interests and a good receipt for his purchase money. It will also be needed in order to deduce title in the future. Once the present deed is of sufficient age to be a root of title, the bare statement that the Trustees are the trustees of the settlement will suffice to protect subsequent purchasers.

2   This may, of course, be the vesting deed.

45

Conveyance by trustees of a settlement to a purchasing tenant for life[1]

This Conveyance dated
is made between:
(1) the Vendors
(2) the Purchaser
(A) For the purposes of the Settled Land Act 1925 the Vendors are the trustees of the settlement referred to in a deed dated *etc*[2] ('the Settlement').
(B) The Purchaser is the tenant for life under the Settlement.
(C) The Settlement relates to [*or* includes] the land and house known as [*postal address*] ('the Property') which is fully described in a conveyance dated *etc*.[3]

1　The Vendors acknowledge the receipt from the Purchaser of
£　　　　　the purchase price of the Property.

2　The Vendors as trustees and in exercise of their powers under section 68 of the Settled Land Act 1925 convey to the Purchaser the fee simple estate in the Property.

Add any appropriate standard clauses[4]

Certificate of value (if applicable)

1   The purpose of the SLA 1925, s 68 is to facilitate transactions between the tenant for life and the trustees of the settlement in relation to assets of the settlement and this precedent is designed for a sale to the tenant for life of land within the settlement, which is one of the authorised transactions. See s 68(1)(a). Under s 68(2) the trustees are given, in addition to their powers as trustees, the powers of the tenant for life to negotiate and complete the authorised transactions. The conveyance will have the same overreaching effect as a conveyance by the tenant for life under s 72. For the position where the tenant for life is one of the trustees, see s 68(3).

2   The deed to be specified is the vesting deed and not the trust instrument.

3   The wording can be adapted if an adequate description of the Property is contained in the Settlement.

4   No acknowledgment for production will be required because the tenant for life will already hold the title deeds.

46

Conveyance to tenant for life on trusts of an an existing settlement[1]

This Conveyance dated
is made between:
(1) the Vendor
(2) the Purchaser
(3) the Trustees

(A) The Trustees are the trustees of the settlement referred to in a vesting deed dated *etc*[2] ('the Vesting Deed').

(B) The Purchaser is the tenant for life under the settlement.

1 The Vendor acknowledges the receipt from the Trustees of £ the purchase price of the land and house known as [*postal address*] ('the Property') which is fully described in a conveyance dated *etc*.

2 By direction of the Purchaser the purchase price has been provided by the Trustees from capital moneys held by them under the settlement.

3 The Vendor as beneficial owner conveys to the Purchaser the fee simple estate in the Property.

4 The Purchaser holds the Property as tenant for life on the same trusts as the land to which the Vesting Deed relates.

5 The power of appointing new trustees of the settlement is vested in the Purchaser during his life [*or as the case may be*].[3]

6 Under the terms of the Vesting Deed the Purchaser has the following powers:

Set out additional powers granted to tenant for life

Add any appropriate standard clauses

Certificate of value (if applicable)

1   This conveyance constitutes a subsidiary vesting deed under SLA 1925, s 10(2) and is governed by that sub-section. An alternative opening is 'This Subsidiary Vesting Deed'.

2   The deed to be specified is the vesting deed and not the trust instrument. Where it is a compound settlement the last principal vesting deed should be specified.

3   It is desirable that the provision for the appointment of new trustees is set out in this deed. Similarly any additional powers available to the tenant for life should be specifically mentioned.

47

Conveyance by statutory owners[1]

This Conveyance dated
is made between:
(1) the Vendors
(2) the Purchaser

1 The Vendors (who are statutory owners within the meaning of the Settled Land Act 1925) acknowledge the receipt from the Purchaser of £   the purchase price of the land and house known as [*postal address*] ('the Property') which is fully described in a conveyance dated *etc*.

2 The Vendors as trustees convey to the Purchaser the fee simple estate in the Property.

Add any appropriate standard clauses

Certificate of value (if applicable)

1   Where there is no tenant for life, the powers of a tenant for life are exercisable by any person of full age on whom those powers are conferred or, if there is none, by the trustees of the settlement. See SLA 1925, s 23. The person entitled to exercise the powers of the tenant for life is called a statutory owner. For the definition of this term, see SLA 1925, s 117(1)(xxvi).

E   Trustees in bankruptcy, liquidators and receivers

48

Conveyance by trustee in bankruptcy[1]

This Conveyance dated
is made between:
(1) the Vendor AB of
as trustee in bankruptcy of CD of
(2) the Purchaser

1   The Vendor acknowledges the receipt from the Purchaser of £
the purchase price of the land and house known as [*postal address*] ('the
Property') which is fully described in a conveyance dated *etc.*

2   The Vendor as trustee[2] conveys to the Purchaser the fee simple estate
in the Property.

Add any appropriate standard clauses

Certificate of value (if applicable)

1   A bankrupt's property vests in the trustee upon his being adjudicated bankrupt: Insolvency Act 1986, s 314. A subsequent annulment of the bankruptcy will not affect the purchaser's title.

2   It is rare, these days, that a trustee in bankruptcy is willing to give any covenants. The words 'as trustee' are inserted more in hope than expectation. The capacity, if any, in which the trustee conveys is, of course, governed by the contract.

49

Conveyance by a company in liquidation—no s 145 order[1]

This Conveyance dated
is made between:
(1) the Company   Limited of *etc* acting by AB its liquidator
(2) the Purchaser

(A) The Company is the owner of the property described in the schedule ('the Property').

For members' voluntary winding up

(B) On [*date*] the Company resolved to be wound up voluntarily and appointed the Liquidator as liquidator.

For creditors' voluntary winding up

(B) on [*date*] the Company resolved to be wound up voluntarily and on [*date*] at a meeting of the creditors of the Company the Liquidator was appointed liquidator.

For compulsory winding up

(B) On [*date*] the High Court of Justice [*or* the   County Court] ordered that the Company be wound up and on [*date*] the Liquidator was appointed as liquidator.

1 The Company acknowledges the receipt from the Purchaser of £   the purchase price of the Property.

2 The Company as beneficial owner conveys to the Purchaser the fee simple estate in the Property.[2]

Add any appropriate standard clauses

Certificate of value (if applicable)

Schedule

Description of Property

Attestation clause[3]

110

1   Insolvency Act 1986, s 91 governs the appointment of a liquidator in a members' voluntary winding up; s 100 in a creditor's winding up and ss 135–140 in a winding up by the Court. It should be noted that the Company's assets do not vest in the liquidator as the assets of a bankrupt vest in his trustee, unless an order is made under s 145, which is comparatively rare. This is so whether the liquidation is voluntary or compulsory. Accordingly, it is the company which conveys, gives the receipt for the purchase money and any acknowledgment for production. The seal of the company is affixed in the presence of the liquidator (in whom the directors' powers are vested) and not in the presence of a director and the secretary.

2   Some contend that the company cannot convey as beneficial owner because the beneficial interest in the company's shares is now vested in the creditors, basing their argument on *Ayerst v C & K (Construction) Limited* [1975] 1 All ER 162. The editor's view is that the company can give beneficial owner covenants although they may be worth very little except for the covenant for further assurances.
These days, a liquidator is rarely willing to give any personal covenants but, if he can be persuaded to give a limited covenant, he should be made a party to the conveyance and the following clause added:
3   The Liquidator covenants with the Purchasers that he has not done or permitted anything which prevents the Company from making this conveyance.
The contract will of course govern the covenants to which the Purchaser is entitled.
3   The liquidator has power to sell the assets of the company and to seal deeds. See Insolvency Act 1986, ss 165–167 and Schedule 4 Part III. The usual form of attestation clause is:
The common seal of the Company was affixed to this deed in the presence of:
Liquidator
It is possible for the liquidator to convey in his own name but this does not accord with modern practice. If he does or, for any reason, the company seal cannot be affixed, the attestation clause is:
Signed sealed and delivered by the Company by AB its liquidator in the presence of:—

50

Conveyance by a company in liquidation—s 145 order in existence[1]

This Conveyance dated
is made between:
(1) the Liquidator
(2) the Purchaser

(A) Prior to [*date in (C)*] Limited ('the Company') was the owner of the property described in the schedule ('the Property').

For members' voluntary winding up

(B) On [*date*] the Company resolved to be wound up voluntarily and appointed the Liquidator as liquidator.

For creditors' voluntary winding-up

(B) On [*date*] the Company resolved to be wound up voluntarily and on [*date*] at a meeting of the creditors of the Company the Liquidator was appointed liquidator.

For compulsory winding up

(B) On [*date*] the High Court of Justice [*or* the County Court] ordered that the Company be wound up and on [*date*] the Liquidator was appointed as liquidator.

(C) On [*date*] an order was made under s 145 of the Insolvency Act 1986 vesting the assets of the Company in the Liquidator.

1 The Liquidator acknowledges the receipt from the Purchaser of £ the purchase price of the Property.

2 The Liquidator conveys to the Purchaser the fee simple estate in the Property.[2]

Add any appropriate standard clauses

Certificate of value (if applicable)

Schedule

Description of Property

Attestation Clause[2]

1   See notes to Precedent 49. An order under Insolvency Act 1986, s 145 is comparatively rare.

2   As the property is vested in the liquidator, no special form of attestation is required and so it will be:

Signed sealed and delivered by the Liquidator in the presence of:

51

Conveyance by receiver appointed under a debenture[1]

This Conveyance dated
is made between:
(1) the Company
(2) the Receiver
(3) the Purchaser

(A) On [*date*] the Company issued a debenture ('the Debenture') charging all its assets including the property described in the schedule ('the Property').

(B) On [*date*] the Receiver was appointed under the provisions of the Debenture to be the administrative receiver of the assets charged.[2]

1 The Receiver acknowledges the receipt from the Purchaser of £   the purchase price of the Property.

2 By direction of the Receiver the Company as beneficial owner conveys to the Purchaser the fee simple estate in the Property.[3]

Add any appropriate standard clauses[4]

Certificate of value (if applicable)

Schedule

Description of Property

1   The assets remain vested in the company and so it is the company which conveys although the receiver gives the receipt for the purchase price. Insolvency Act 1986, s 42 and Schedule 1 give the receiver express powers to sell the assets charged, to execute deeds in the name of the company and to use the company seal. The usual form of attestation clause is:

The common seal of the Company was affixed to this deed in the presence of:
Receiver

Where the company goes into liquidation after a receiver has been appointed, the right of the receiver to act as agent for the company ceases (s 44) although he still has power to dispose of assets charged by the debenture. Where a receivership and a liquidation exist contemporaneously, the following attestation clause should be used:

Signed sealed and delivered by X Limited (in liquidation) by AB its receiver pursuant to powers granted to him in clause [*number*] of the Debenture in favour of LM Bank Plc in the presence of:

This wording is accepted by the Land Registry for use in transfers where a receivership and a liquidation co-exist. It is very likely that the debenture will give the receiver express power to sell and to execute deeds in the name of the company but, if he should be dependent on the powers granted by Insolvency Act, s 42, it is suggested the following attestation clause be used:

Signed sealed and delivered by X Limited (in liquidation) by the Liquidator pursuant to the powers vested in him by the Insolvency Act 1986 in the presence of:

Even if the conveyance is sealed by the company, it is desirable that it be executed by the receiver as evidence of the direction given by him in clause 2 and it must be executed by him if it contains a covenant by him. See note 3.

2   As the appointment is under a debenture, the receiver will be an administrative receiver. See Insolvency Act 1986, s 29(2).

3   Unless the contract provides otherwise, the Company should convey as beneficial owner. Usually, a receiver is unwilling to give any personal covenant but if he can be persuaded to give a limited covenant, the following clause should be added to the deed:

3   The Receiver covenants with the Purchaser that he has not done or permitted anything which prevents the Company from making this conveyance

4   Any acknowledgment for the production of earlier title deeds should be given by the company. An acknowledgment will be required in respect of the debenture. The company is not entitled to possession of the debenture and so this acknowledgment ought to be given by the debenture holder. It is preferable that the debenture holder give a separate acknowledgment rather than his being made a party to the deed for the sole purpose of giving the acknowledgment.

52

Conveyance by administrator appointed under an administration order[1]

This Conveyance dated
is made between:
(1) the Company
(2) the Administrator
(3) the Purchaser

(A) Prior to [date of administration order] the Company was the owner of the property described in the schedule ('the Property').

(B) On [date] the High Court of Justice [or the   County Court] made an administration order appointing the Administrator as administrator of the Company.

1 The Administrator acknowledges the receipt from Purchaser of £   the purchase price of the Property.

2 By direction of the Administrator the Company as beneficial owner conveys to the Purchaser the fee simple estate in the Property.[2]

Add any appropriate standard clauses[3]

Certificate of value (if applicable)

Schedule

Description of the Property.

1   The assets remain vested in the company and so it is the company which conveys although the administrator gives the receipt for the purchase price. Insolvency Act 1986, s 14 and Schedule 1 give the administrator express powers to sell the assets, to execute deeds in the name of the company and to use the company seal. The usual form of attestation clause is:

The common seal of the Company was affixed to this deed in the presence of:

Administrator

It is desirable that the conveyance be executed by the administrator as evidence of the direction given by him in clause 2 and it must be executed by him if it contains a covenant by him. See note 2.

2   Unless the contract provides otherwise, the Company should convey as beneficial owner. Usually, an administrator is unwilling to give any personal covenant but if he can be persuaded to give a limited covenant, the following clause should be added to the deed:

3   The Administrator covenants with the Purchaser that he has not done or permitted anything which prevents the Company from making this Conveyance.

3   Any acknowledgment for the production of earlier title deeds should be given by the company.

F   Friendly societies and unincorporated associations

53

Conveyance to trustees of a friendly society or a branch of a friendly society

This Conveyance dated
is made between:
(1) the Vendor
(2) the Purchasers being the persons whose names and addresses are set out in the first schedule and who are the present trustees of the registered friendly society known as   ('the Society').[1]

1   The Vendor acknowledges the receipt from the Purchaser of
£   the purchase price of the property described in the second schedule ('the Property').

2   The Vendor as beneficial owner conveys to the Purchasers the fee simple estate in the Property.

3   The Purchasers declare:

   (a) This Conveyance is made with the consent of [the Committee of] the Society.[2]

   (b) They hold the Property in trust for the Society and its members in accordance with its rules.

Add any appropriate standard clauses

Certificate of value (if applicable)

First Schedule
Names and addresses of the Purchasers

Second Schedule
Description of Property

1   If the purchasers are a branch of the friendly society, the wording should be adapted and it would probably be better to describe the branch as 'the Branch' or something similar rather than as 'the Society'.

2   Friendly Societies Act 1896, ss 44 and 47 provide that, if the society or branch rules give the appropriate power, funds may be invested in the purchase of land with the consent of the committee or a majority of the members present and entitled to vote at a meeting of the society or branch.

54

Conveyance by trustees of a friendly society or a branch of a friendly society

This Conveyance dated
is made between:
(1) the Vendors being the persons whose names and addresses are set out in the first schedule and who are the present trustees of the registered friendly society known as ('the Society').[1]
(2) the Purchaser

1 The Vendors acknowledge the receipt from the Purchaser of £ the purchase price of the property described in the second schedule ('the Property').

2 The Vendors as trustees convey to the Purchaser the fee simple estate in the Property.

3 The Vendors warrant that they have complied with all formalities necessary for effecting this sale.[2]

Add any appropriate standard clauses

Certificate of value (if applicable)

First Schedule
Names and addresses of the Vendors

Second Schedule
Description of Property

1   If the vendor is a branch of the friendly society the wording should be adapted and it would probably be better to describe the branch as 'the Branch' or something similar rather than as 'the Society'.

2   Friendly Societies Act 1896, s 47 permits a society to sell and provides that a purchaser shall not be concerned to enquire as to the authority of the trustee to sell and that their receipt shall be a discharge. The purchaser must, however, be satisfied that the trustees are properly appointed. Section 25 provides that the appointment shall be at a meeting of the society or branch by a resolution of the majority of the members present and entitled to vote. A copy of the resolution signed by the trustees appointed must be sent to the Registrar of Friendly Societies. The Purchaser should therefore require production of a copy of the filed resolution together with a copy of the rules of the society. On the death removal or retirement of a trustee, the property will (under s 50) vest in the continuing trustees or in the personal representative of the surviving trustee.

The purchaser will only be entitled to this warranty, if the contract so provides or the trustees subsequently agree to its inclusion. It is doubtful whether the trustees will be willing to warrant 'jointly and severally.'

55

Conveyance to an unincorporated association[1]

This Conveyance dated
is made between:
(1) the Vendor
(2) the Purchasers being the persons whose names and addresses are set out in the first schedule and who are the present trustees of
('the Association').

1 The Vendor acknowledges the receipt from the Purchasers of £   the purchase price of the property described in the second schedule ('the Property').

2 The Vendor as beneficial owner conveys to the Purchasers the fee simple estate in the Property.

3 The Purchasers declare that:

(a) They hold the Property as trustees for sale in trust for the Association and its members in accordance with its rules;

(b) They shall deal with the Property in such manner as the Association shall from time to time direct;

(c) They shall have powers to deal with it equal to those of a sole beneficial owner;

(d) A purchaser from the trustees for the time being shall not be concerned to enquire what directions have been given to the trustees by the Association.

Add any appropriate standard clauses

Certificate of value (if applicable)

First Schedule

Names and addresses of Trustees

Second Schedule

Description of the Property

1   Practitioners need not be reminded of the problems that arise from unincorporated associations holding property. The members of the association usually wish the trustees to deal with the property in accordance with their wishes and to act in accordance with lawful directions given to them. On the other hand, purchasers from trustees do not wish to have to verify what directions have been given or the validity of those directions. Nor do they wish to have to investigate the rules of the association and amendments to them that may have taken place since the acquisition of the property. It is believed that the form of this precedent overcomes this difficulty. Clause 3(c) has been included principally to enable the trustees to have unrestricted powers to mortgage.

The failure to replace trustees who have died, resigned or ceased to be interested in the association also creates problems. Particularly if the property acquired is of substantial value, consideration ought to be given to creating a company limited by shares or guarantee to act as trustee of the property of the association.

G   Properties subject to rentcharges

56

Conveyance of property subject to a rentcharge[1]

This Conveyance dated
is made between:
(1) the Vendor
(2) the Purchaser

1 The Vendor acknowledges the receipt from the Purchaser of £   the purchase price of the land and house known as [*postal address*] ('the Property') which is fully described in a conveyance dated *etc* ('the Rentcharge Deed').

2 The Vendor as beneficial owner conveys to the Purchaser the fee simple estate in the Property.

3 The Property is subject to a yearly rentcharge of £   made payable by the Rentcharge Deed and to such covenants and restrictions contained in that deed as are still effective.

Add any appropriate standard clauses

Certificate of value (if applicable)

1   Where the Conveyance is for valuable consideration, LPA 1925, s 77(1) (A) implies covenants for the payment of rent, for the performance of the grantees covenants and for indemnity.

Where the Conveyance is not for valuable consideration and covenants are desired the following clause should be used:

> The same covenants shall be implied in this conveyance as if it had been for valuable consideration

It is important that the Vendor obtains a covenant for the payment of rent, the performance of covenants and for indemnity, because he himself remains liable on any covenants into which he has entered notwithstanding the transfer of the whole of his interest in the property.

57

Conveyance of property subject to a rentcharge to the owner of the rentcharge so as to extinguish it[1]

This Conveyance dated
is made between:
(1) the Vendor
(2) the Purchaser

1 The Vendor acknowledges the receipt from the Purchaser of £ the purchase price of the land and house known as [*postal address*] ('the Property') which is fully described in a conveyance dated *etc* ('the Rentcharge Deed').

2 The Vendor as beneficial owner conveys to the Purchaser the fee simple estate in the Property.

3 The Property is subject to a yearly rentcharge of £ ('the Rentcharge') made payable by the Rentcharge Deed and to such covenants and restrictions contained in that deed as are still effective.

4 The Purchaser who is the owner of the Rentcharge declares that from the date of this deed the Property:
   (a) shall cease to be charged with the payment of the Rentcharge;
   (b) shall no longer be subject to [the positive covenants] *or* [the covenants and restrictions] contained in the Rentcharge Deed.[2]

Add any appropriate standard clauses

Certificate of value (if applicable)

1   See note 1 to preceding precedent.

2   If the purchaser wishes to keep the rentcharge alive, clause 4 should be omitted. It used to be common practice to extinguish the rentcharge because the purchaser could always create a new rentcharge on a sale of the property if he so wished. Now that no new rentcharges can be created, a purchaser may wish not to extinguish the rentcharge in the conveyance to him but to leave his options open and, on a future sale, either extinguish the rentcharge or sell the property subject to the rentcharge.

By clause 3 the vendor conveys the property to the purchaser subject to the rentcharge and to the covenants and restrictions affecting the property. By clause 4 the purchaser releases the property from the rentcharge and the covenants. As rentcharge owner the purchaser can release the property from the rentcharge and from those covenants that attached to the rentcharge for the purpose of securing its payment. There may, however, be restrictive covenants from which the purchaser is legally incapable of releasing the property because, for example, they are expressed to be for the benefit of adjoining land or are 'building scheme' covenants. If he purports to do so and subsequently conveys the unencumbered property as beneficial owner, he may be exposing himself to liabilities to his purchaser in the event of his purported release of the restrictive covenants being ineffective. For this reason, clause 4(b) contains an alternative.

It is for the purchaser to decide whether he is legally capable of effecting the release; the vendor has no part in it. Certainly he would be unwise to purport to release the restrictive covenants if they are registered as D(ii) Land Charges because he will probably be unable to obtain the removal of the registration. The reason for this is that the Registrar contends (and rightly so it is submitted) that the owner of a rentcharge cannot release restrictive covenants that are expressed to be for the benefit of adjoining land unless he can also establish that he owns the entirety of the land intended to be benefited by those covenants.

58

Conveyance of part of property affected by a rentcharge— rent apportioned[1]

This Conveyance dated
is made between:
(1) the Vendor
(2) the Purchaser

1 The Vendor acknowledges the receipt from the Purchaser of £ the purchase price of the land and house known as [*postal address*] ('the Property Conveyed') which is fully described in the first schedule.

2 The Vendor as beneficial owner conveys to the Purchaser the fee simple estate in the Property Conveyed.

If a plan is used
3 (a) The Property Conveyed and the land shown edged [*blue*] on the attached plan ('the Retained Premises') together comprise the whole of the property conveyed by a conveyance dated *etc* ('the Rentcharge Deed') and are subject to a yearly rentcharge of £ made payable by the Rentcharge Deed.

(b) The Vendor and the Purchaser agree that from the date of this deed the yearly rentcharge of £ is apportioned between the Property Conveyed and the Retained Premises so that the Property Conveyed is subject to a yearly rentcharge of £ and the Retained Premises are subject to a yearly rentcharge of £ .

If a plan is not used
3 (a) The whole of the property conveyed by a conveyance dated *etc* ('the Rentcharge Deed') which includes the Property Conveyed is subject to a yearly rentcharge of £ made payable by the Rentcharge Deed.

(b) The Vendor and the Purchaser agree that from the date of this deed the yearly rentcharge of £ is apportioned between the Property Conveyed and the remainder of the land conveyed by the Rentcharge Deed ('the Retained Premises') so that the Property Conveyed is subject to a yearly rentcharge of £ and the Retained Premises are subject to a yearly rentcharge of £ .

1   Please refer to the Appendix (pp 299ff) for observations of general application to sales-off and the apportionment of rentcharges.

4   The Vendor and the Purchaser declare that from the date of this deed:

    (a)   the Property Conveyed stands charged with the payment of all money which may become payable under the covenants on the part of the Purchaser implied by the Law of Property Act 1925;[2]

    (b)   the Retained Premises stand charged with the payment of all money which may become payable under the covenants on the part of the Vendor implied by the Law of Property Act 1925;[2]

    (c)   any wall fence or hedge separating the Property Conveyed from the Retained Premises shall be a party structure to be repaired and maintained at the equally shared expense of its owners;

    (d)   any sewers drains electricity cables gas pipes gutters downspouts or similar conduits serving both the Property Conveyed and the Retained Premises shall continue to be used as they were prior to the date of this deed [and shall be repaired and maintained at the equally shared expense of the owners of the Property Conveyed and of the Retained Premises];[3]

    (e)   no rights of way over the Retained Premises shall be implied in this deed;[4]

    (f)   section 62 of the Law of Property Act 1925 shall not apply to this deed.[4]

5   The Property Conveyed is subject to such covenants and restrictions contained in the Rentcharge Deed as are still effective and relate to it.

6   The Vendor undertakes to keep safe the documents listed in the second schedule and acknowledges the right of the Purchaser to their production and to the supply of copies.

Add any appropriate standard clauses

Certificate of value (if applicable)

First Schedule
The land and house known as [*postal address*] shown edged red on the attached plan.
or appropriate verbal description if a plan is not used
There is excepted from this conveyance any easement quasi-easement or right that prior to the date of this deed was enjoyed by the Vendor for the benefit of the Retained Premises and which continues to be necessary to the reasonable enjoyment of the Retained Premises.[5]

Second Schedule
List of documents to which the acknowledgment relates.

2   Strictly speaking this subclause could be omitted because clause 3 brings into operation LPA 1925, s 190.

3   Most draftsmen make provision for the cost of repairing and maintaining party structures to be borne by the parties in equal shares, as in the precedent. The cost of rebuilding, say, a party wall could be expensive. Moreover, neither party is likely to undertake the work without the other contributing to its cost. The same considerations do not apply to conduits. Some draftsmen prefer to make no provision for their maintenance, relying on the fact that the owner of each house is likely to undertake the repair of conduits on or under his own property and that, in many cases, it is hardly worth seeking a contribution. Different considerations would apply however to, say, a private sewer serving the two houses. In some circumstances, it may be proper to provide for the contribution to repairs to be in unequal shares. Whenever possible, however, it is preferable to define the contribution of the parties rather than make provision for the payment of a 'fair proportion of the cost' which can be a fruitful source of dispute in the future.

4   It is likely that this provision will be required to be adapted to the circumstances. It has been inserted to remind the draftsman of the need to give consideration to these matters. See Appendix pp 299ff.

5   Please refer to the Appendix (pp 299ff) for observations concerning rights to be excepted.

59

Conveyance of part of property affected by a rentcharge where the rent has previously been apportioned[1]

This Conveyance dated
is made between:
(1) the Vendor
(2) the Purchaser

1 The Vendor acknowledges the receipt from the Purchaser of £ the purchase price of the land and house known as [*postal address*] ('the Property') which is fully described in a conveyance dated *etc*.[2]

2 The Vendor as beneficial owner conveys to the Purchaser the fee simple estate in the Property.

3 The Property is subject to:

(a) an apportioned yearly rent of £ made payable by a conveyance dated *etc* ('the Conveyance');

(b) such covenants and restrictions contained in a conveyance dated *etc* [*the rentcharge deed*] as are still effective and relate to the Property;

(c) the covenants and charges by [*the grantee of the Conveyance*] implied or contained in the Conveyance.

Add any appropriate standard clauses

Certificate of value (if applicable)

1   Where the rent reserved by the rentcharge deed has been apportioned since 1925, the purchaser will take the property conveyed by this deed subject to but with the benefit of the covenants and charges relating to the apportionment contained or implied in the apportionment deed (LPA 1925, ss 77(5) and 79). Clause 3(c) is not therefore strictly necessary. It is preferable, however, that this deed should show the restrictions to which the property is subject, but it is not so important that the deed should reveal that the purchaser has the benefit of certain covenants by statute.

2   It is quite likely that the conveyance containing a description of the Property will be the deed that apportioned the rentcharge. In this event, it will be defined in clause 1 as 'the Conveyance' with a consequential amendment to clause 3(a).

60

Conveyance of part of property affected by a rentcharge the part conveyed being exonerated from the whole of the rent[1]

This Conveyance dated
is made between:
(1) the Vendor
(2) the Purchaser

1 The Vendor acknowledges the receipt from the Purchaser of £　　　the purchase price of the land and house known as [*postal address*] ('the Property Conveyed') which is fully described in the first schedule.

2 The Vendor as beneficial owner conveys to the Purchaser the fee simple estate in the Property Conveyed.

If a plan is used
3 (a) The Property Conveyed and the land shown edged [*blue*] on the attached plan ('the Retained Premises') together comprise the whole of the property conveyed by a conveyance dated *etc* ('the Rentcharge Deed') and are subject to a yearly rentcharge of £　　　made payable by the Rentcharge Deed.

(b) The Vendor and the Purchaser agree that from the date of this deed the whole of the yearly rentcharge of £　　　shall be charged on the Retained Premises in exoneration of the Property Conveyed.

If a plan is not used
3 (a) The whole of the property conveyed by a conveyance dated *etc* ('the Rentcharge Deed') which includes the Property Conveyed is subject to a yearly rentcharge of £　　　made payable by the Rentcharge Deed.

(b) The Vendor and the Purchaser agree that from the date of this deed the Property Conveyed shall be exonerated from the yearly rentcharge of £　　　the whole of which shall be charged on the remainder of the land conveyed by the Rentcharge Deed ('the Retained Premises').

4 The Property Conveyed is subject to such covenants and restrictions contained in the Rentcharge Deed as are still effective and relate to it.

1   Please refer to the Appendix (pp 299ff) for observations of general application to sales-off and the apportionment of rentcharges.

5   As a variant of the covenants referred to in section 77(1)(B) of the Law of Property Act 1925:[2]

(a) The Vendor covenants with the Purchaser to pay the yearly rentcharge of £   and to perform and observe such covenants and restrictions contained in the Rentcharge Deed as are still effective and relate to the Retained Premises and to indemnify the Purchaser against any liability resulting from a breach of this covenant;

(b) The Purchaser covenants with the Vendor to perform and observe such covenants and restrictions contained in the Rentcharge Deed as are still effective and relate to the Property Conveyed and to indemnify the Vendor against any liability resulting from a breach of this covenant.

6   The Vendor and the Purchaser agree that from the date of this deed:

(a) the Property Conveyed stands charged with the payment of all money which may become payable under the covenant on the part of the Purchaser contained in this deed;

(b) the Retained Premises stand charged with the payment of all money which may become payable under the covenant on the part of the Vendor contained in this deed;

(c) any wall fence or hedge separating the Property Conveyed from the Retained Premises shall be a party structure to be repaired and maintained at the equally shared expense of its owners;[3]

(d) any sewers drains electricity cables gas pipes gutters downspouts or similar conduits serving both the Property Conveyed and the Retained Premises shall continue to be used as they were prior to the date of this deed [and shall be repaired and maintained at the equally shared expense of the owners of the Property Conveyed and of the Retained Premises];[3]

(e) no right of way over the Retained Premises shall be implied in this deed;[4]

(f) section 62 of the Law of Property Act 1925 shall not apply to this deed.[4]

7   The Vendor undertakes to keep safe the documents listed in the second schedule and acknowledges the right of the Purchaser to their production and to the supply of copies.

Add any appropriate standard clauses

Certificate of value (if applicable)

2   Section 77(2) is obscure but it appears that a covenant is implied on the part of the vendor for payment of the entire rentcharge, for the performance of the covenants and restrictions relating to the retained property and for indemnity. It is not clear from that section, however, that any covenant is implied on the part of the purchaser for the performance of the covenants and restrictions affecting the property conveyed. Conveyancers are not agreed upon whether a covenant is implied or not and the general practice is to insert an express covenant by the purchaser. This practice has been followed here. An express covenant by the vendor has also been included, partly because of the purchaser's express covenant and partly because of the inept wording of section 77(2). Both covenants are expressed to be variants of the covenants referred to in section 77(1)(B) so as to obtain the benefit of the provisions of section 77(6) by virtue of section 77(4).

3   Most draftsmen make provision for the cost of repairing and maintaining party structures to be borne by the parties in equal shares, as in the precedent. The cost of rebuilding, say, a party wall could be expensive. Moreover, neither party is likely to undertake the work without the other contributing to its cost. The same considerations do not apply to conduits. Some draftsmen prefer to make no provision for their maintenance, relying on the fact that the owner of each house is likely to undertake the repair of conduits on or under his own property and that, in many cases, it is hardly worth seeking a contribution. Different considerations would apply however to, say, a private sewer serving the two houses. In some circumstances, it may be proper to provide for the contribution to repairs to be in unequal shares. Whenever possible, however, it is preferable to define the contribution of the parties rather than make provision for the payment of a 'fair proportion of the cost' which can be a fruitful source of dispute in the future.

4   It is likely that this provision requires to be adapted to the circumstances. It has been inserted to remind the draftsman of the need to give consideration to these matters. See Appendix (pp 299ff).

First Schedule

The land and house known as [*postal address*] shown edged red on the attached plan

or appropriate verbal description if a plan is not used

There is excepted from this conveyance any easement quasi-easement or right that prior to the date of this deed was enjoyed by the Vendor for the benefit of the Retained Premises and which continues to be necessary to the reasonable enjoyment of the Retained Premises.[5]

Second Schedule

List of documents to which the acknowledgment relates

5   Please refer to the Appendix (p 299ff) for observations concerning rights to be excepted.

61

Conveyance of part of property affected by a rentcharge the part conveyed being charged with the whole of the rent[1]

This Conveyance dated
is made between
(1) the Vendor
(2) the Purchaser

1 The Vendor acknowledges the receipt from the Purchaser of £ the purchase price of the land and house known as [*postal address*] ('the Property Conveyed') which is fully described in the first schedule.

2 The Vendor as beneficial owner conveys to the Purchaser the fee simple estate in the Property Conveyed.

If a plan is used

3 (a) The Property Conveyed and the land shown edged [*blue*] on the attached plan ('the Retained Premises') together comprise the whole of the property conveyed by a conveyance dated *etc* ('the Rentcharge Deed') and are subject to a yearly rentcharge of £ made payable by the Rentcharge Deed.

   (b) The Vendor and the Purchaser agree that from the date of this deed the whole of the yearly rentcharge of £ shall be charged on the Property Conveyed in exoneration of the Retained Premises.

If a plan is not used

3 (a) The whole of the property conveyed by a conveyance dated *etc* ('the Rentcharge Deed') which includes the Property Conveyed is subject to a yearly rentcharge of £ made payable by the Rentcharge Deed.

   (b) The Vendor and the Purchaser agree that from the date of this deed the whole of the yearly rentcharge of £ shall be charged on the Property Conveyed in exoneration of the remainder of the premises conveyed by the Rentcharge Deed ('the Retained Premises').

4 The Property Conveyed is subject to such covenants and restrictions contained in the Rentcharge Deed as are still effective and relate to the Property Conveyed.

1   Please refer to the Appendix (pp 299ff) for observations of general application to sales-off.

5 As a variant of the covenants referred to in section 77(1)(B) of the Law of Property Act 1925:[2]

(a) The Purchaser covenants with the Vendor to pay the yearly rentcharge of £   and to perform and observe such covenants and restrictions contained in the Rentcharge Deed as are still effective and relate to the Property Conveyed and to indemnify the Vendor against any liability resulting from a breach of this covenant;

(b) The Vendor covenants with the Purchaser to perform and observe such covenants and restrictions contained in the Rentcharge Deed as are still effective and relate to the Retained Premises and to indemnify the Purchaser against any liability resulting from a breach of this covenant.

6 The Vendor and the Purchaser agree that from the date of this deed:

(a) the Property Conveyed stands charged with the payment of all money which may become payable under the covenant on the part of the Purchaser contained in this deed;

(b) the Retained Premises stand charged with the payment of all money which may become payable under the covenant on the part of the Vendor contained in this deed;

(c) any wall fence or hedge separating the Property Conveyed from the Retained Premises shall be a party structure to be repaired and maintained at the equally shared expense of its owners;

(d) any sewer drains electricity cables gas pipes gutters downspouts or similar conduits serving both the Property Conveyed and the Retained Premises shall continue to be used as they were prior to the date of this deed [and shall be repaired and maintained at the equally shared expense of the owners of the Property Conveyed and of the Retained Premises][3]

(e) no right of way over the Retained Premises shall be implied in this deed;[4]

(f) section 62 of the Law of Property Act 1925 shall not apply to this deed.[4]

7 The Vendor undertakes to keep safe the documents listed in the second schedule and acknowledges the right of the Purchaser to their production and to the supply of copies.

Add any appropriate standard clauses

Certificate of value (if applicable)

2 See note 2 to preceding precedent. Here the converse is the case. It is fairly clear that a covenant is implied on the part of the purchaser but it is not clear that a covenant is implied on the part of the vendor.

3 Most draftsmen make provision for the cost of repairing and maintaining party structures to be borne by the parties in equal shares, as in the precedent. The cost of rebuilding, say, a party wall could be expensive. Moreover, neither party is likely to undertake the work without the other contributing to its cost. The same considerations do not apply to conduits. Some draftsmen prefer to make no provision for their maintenance, relying on the fact that the owner of each house is likely to undertake the repair of conduits on or under his own property and that, in many cases, it is hardly worth seeking a contribution. Different considerations would apply however to, say, a private sewer serving the two houses. In some circumstances, it may be proper to provide for the contribution to repairs to be in unequal shares. Whenever possible, however, it is preferable to define the contribution of the parties rather than make provision for the payment of a 'fair proportion of the cost' which can be a fruitful source of dispute in the future.

4 It is likely that this provision will require to be adapted to the circumstances. It has been inserted to remind the draftsman to give consideration to these matters. See Appendix (pp 299ff).

First Schedule

The land and house known as [*postal address*] shown edged red on the attached plan.

or appropriate verbal description if a plan is not used

There is excepted and reserved from this Conveyance any easement quasi-easement or right that prior to the date of this deed was enjoyed by the Vendor for the benefit of the Retained Premises and which continues to be necessary to the reasonable enjoyment of the Retained Premises.[4]

Second Schedule

List of documents to which the acknowledgment relates

4   Please refer to the Appendix for observations concerning rights to be excepted.

62

Conveyance of residue of property affected by a rentcharge where there has been a previous sale of part and rent apportioned

This Conveyance dated
is made between:
(1) the Vendor
(2) the Purchaser

1 The Vendor acknowledges the receipt from the Purchaser of £   the purchase price of the land and house known as [*postal address*] ('the Property') which is fully described in the schedule.

2 The Vendor as beneficial owner conveys to the Purchaser the fee simple estate in the Property.

3 The Property is subject to:

(a) an apportioned yearly rentcharge of £   made payable by a conveyance dated *etc* ('the Conveyance') and to the covenants and charges by [*the grantor of that deed*] implied or contained in that conveyance;[1]

(b) such covenants and restrictions contained in a conveyance dated *etc* [*the original rentcharge deed*] as are still effective and relate to the Property.

Add any appropriate standard clauses

Certificate of value (if applicable)

Schedule

Description of the Property[2]

1 Where the rent reserved by the rentcharge deed has been apportioned since 1925, the purchaser will take the property conveyed by this deed subject to but with the benefit of the covenants and charges relating to the apportionment contained or implied in the apportionment deed (LPA 1925, ss 77(5) and 79). Clause 3(c) is not therefore strictly necessary. It is preferable, however, that this deed should show the restrictions to which the property is subject, but it is not so important that the deed should reveal that the purchaser has the benefit of certain covenants by statute.

2 What rights are granted and excepted will be governed by the provisions of the earlier sale-off. Perhaps a provision along the following lines would be suitable:
This conveyance includes the rights expressed to be excepted from the Conveyance but there are excepted from this conveyance the rights expressly or impliedly granted by the Conveyance that affect the Property.

63

Conveyance of part of property affected by a rentcharge where there has been a previous sale-off at an apportioned rent and there is a further apportionment on the present sale[1]

This Conveyance dated
is made between:
(1) the Vendor
(2) the Purchaser

1 The Vendor acknowledges the receipt from the Purchaser of £ the purchase price of the land and house known as [*postal address*] ('the Property Conveyed') which is fully described in the first schedule.

2 The Vendor as beneficial owner conveys to the Purchaser the fee simple estate in the Property Conveyed.

3 (a) The Property Conveyed and the premises described in the second schedule ('the Retained Premises') are together subject to an apportioned yearly rentcharge of £ which is part of the yearly rentcharge of £ made payable by a conveyance dated *etc* ('the Rentcharge Deed').

    (b) The Vendor and the Purchaser agree that from the date of this deed the apportioned yearly rentcharge of £ is further apportioned so that the Property Conveyed is subject to a yearly rentcharge of £ and the Retained Premises are subject to a yearly rentcharge of £ .

4 The Vendor and Purchaser declare that from the date of this deed:

    (a) the Property Conveyed stands charged with the payment of all money which may become payable under the covenants on the part of the Purchaser implied by the Law of Property Act 1925;[2]

    (b) the Retained Premises stand charged with the payment of all money which may become payable under the covenants on the part of the Vendor implied by the Law of Property Act 1925;[2]

    (c) any wall fence or hedge separating the Property Conveyed from the Retained Premises shall be a party structure to be repaired and maintained at the equally shared expense of its owners;

    (d) any sewers drains electricity cables gas pipes gutters downspouts and similar conduits serving both the Property Conveyed and the Retained Premises shall continue to be used as they were

1   Please refer to the Appendix (pp 299ff) for observations of general application to sales-off and the apportionment of rentcharges.

2   Strictly speaking this clause could be omitted because clause 3 brings into operation LPA 1925, s 190.

prior to the date of this deed [and shall be repaired and maintained at the equally shared expense of the owners of the Property Conveyed and of the Retained Premises];[3]

(e) no right of way over the Retained Premises shall be implied in this deed;[4]

(f) section 62 of the Law of Property Act 1925 shall not apply to this deed.[4]

5   The Property Conveyed is subject to:[5]

(a) such covenants and restrictions contained in the Rentcharge Deed as are still effective and relate to the Property Conveyed;

(b) the agreements declarations covenants and charges implied or contained in an assignment dated *etc* whereby part of the land comprised in the Rentcharge Deed was conveyed subject to an apportioned yearly rentcharge of £   .

6   The Vendor undertakes to keep safe the documents listed in the third schedule and acknowledges the right of the Purchaser to their production and to the supply of copies.

Add any appropriate standard clauses

Certificate of value (if applicable)

First Schedule
Description of the Property Conveyed[6]

Second Schedule
The land and houses known as [*postal addresses of the Retained Premises*]

Third Schedule
List of documents to which the acknowledgment relates

3   Most draftsmen make provision for the cost of repairing and maintaining party structures to be borne by the parties in equal shares, as in the precedent. The cost of rebuilding, say, a party wall could be expensive. Moreover, neither party is likely to undertake the work without the other contributing to its cost. The same considerations do not apply to conduits. Some draftsmen prefer to make no provision for their maintenance, relying on the fact that the owner of each house is likely to undertake the repair of conduits on or under his own property and that, in many cases, it is hardly worth seeking a contribution. Different considerations would apply however to, say, a private sewer serving the two houses. In some circumstances, it may be proper to provide for the contribution to repairs to be in unequal shares. Whenever possible, however, it is preferable to define the contribution of the parties rather than make provision for the payment of a 'fair proportion of the cost' which can be a fruitful source of dispute in the future.

4   It is likely that this provision will require to be adapted to the circumstances. It has been inserted to remind the draftsman to give consideration to these matters. See Appendix (pp 299ff).

5   Where there has been more than one sale-off, this precedent can easily be adapted by amending clause 5(b) to read:

   (b) the agreements declarations covenants and charges by each of the grantors implied or contained in the [four] conveyances specified on the third schedule by which other houses comprised in the Rentcharge Deed have been sold-off as set out in that schedule.

In clause 6, the acknowledgment will then relate to the documents listed in the fourth schedule.

6   Please refer to the Appendix (pp 299ff) for observations concerning rights to be excepted.

64

Conveyance of the residue of property affected by a rentcharge with the benefit of second rentcharges created by previous sales-off

This Conveyance dated
is made between:
(1) the Vendor
(2) the Purchaser

1 The Vendor acknowledges the receipt from the Purchaser of
£   the purchase price of the property conveyed by this deed.

2 The Vendor as beneficial owner conveys to the Purchaser:

(a) the fee simple estate in the property described in the first schedule ('the Property');[1]

(b) the [three] yearly rentcharges created by the conveyances specified in the second schedule ('the Scheduled Conveyances');

(c) all powers and remedies for securing the payment of the rentcharges and the benefit of all covenants contained in the Scheduled Conveyances.

3 The Property is subject to a yearly rentcharge of £   created by a conveyance dated *etc* ('the Rentcharge Deed') and to such covenants and restrictions contained in that deed as are still effective and relate to the Property.

Add any appropriate standard clauses

Certificate of value (if applicable)

First Schedule
Description of Property being the whole of the property conveyed by the Rentcharge Deed except those parts conveyed by the Scheduled Conveyances.[2]

Second Schedule

Date of deed	Property conveyed	Parties	Rentcharge

1　The benefit of the restrictive covenants referred to in the Scheduled Conveyances will be annexed to the property conveyed by this deed because it adjoins the property conveyed by the Scheduled Conveyances. An express assignment of the restrictive covenants is not therefore necessary. Nevertheless there is no need for the covenants in clause 2(c) to be restricted to positive covenants.

2　The words to be added to the description of the property conveyed are intended to meet the view that the vendor should ensure that no part of the property conveyed by the original rentcharge deed remains vested in him.

65

Conveyance of a rentcharge

This Conveyance dated
is made between:
(1) the Vendor
(2) the Purchaser

1 The Vendor acknowledges the receipt from the Purchaser of £   the purchase price of the rentcharge conveyed by this deed.

2 The Vendor as beneficial owner conveys to the Purchaser the yearly rentcharge of £   created by a conveyance dated *etc* ('the Rentcharge Deed') and charged on the property conveyed by the Rentcharge Deed together with all powers and remedies for securing payment of the rentcharge and the benefit of such covenants contained in the Rentcharge Deed as are capable of being conveyed by the Vendor.[1]

Add any appropriate standard clauses

Certificate of value (if applicable)

1   Covenants that are designed for the security of the rentcharge can be conveyed to the purchaser but restrictive covenants, expressed to be for the benefit of adjoining land, cannot be transferred with the rentcharge and, in any case, could not be enforced by the purchaser. In some rentcharge deeds, it was quite common for no distinction to be made between restrictive covenants and rentcharge covenants. Moreover, some modern conveyancers take the view that certain restrictive covenants can also be security for the rentcharge. In order that this precedent may be of general application the vendor is expressed to convey the benefit of such of the covenants contained in the rentcharge deed 'as are capable of being conveyed'. Where the vendor is also the owner of adjoining land which has the benefit of the restrictive covenants contained in the original rentcharge deed it should be made clear that the vendor is not purporting to assign the benefit of the restrictive covenants by adding, at the end of the clause, '(other than restrictive covenants)'.

66

Conveyance of a rentcharge to the owner of the property charged so as to extinguish the rent

This Conveyance dated
is made between:
(1) the Vendor
(2) the Purchaser

1 The Vendor acknowledges the receipt from the Purchaser of £   the purchase price of the rentcharge conveyed by this deed.

2 The Vendor as beneficial owner conveys to the Purchaser the yearly rentcharge of £   created by a conveyance dated *etc* ('the Rentcharge Deed') and charged on the property conveyed by the Rentcharge Deed ('the Property') together with all powers and remedies for securing the payment of the rentcharge and the benefit of such covenants contained in the Rentcharge Deed as are capable of being conveyed by the Vendor.[1]

3 The Purchaser who is the owner of the Property declares that from the date of this deed the Property:

(a) shall cease to be charged with the payment of the rentcharge;

(b) shall no longer be subject to [the positive covenants] *or* [the covenants and restrictions] contained in the Rentcharge Deed.[2]

Add any appropriate standard clauses

Certificate of value (if applicable)

1   See note 1 to preceding precedent.

2   By this clause, the purchaser releases the property from the rentcharge and the covenants. The purchaser, as the new owner of the rentcharge, can release the property from the rentcharge and from the covenants relating to its payment. There may, however, be restrictive covenants from which the purchaser cannot release the property because, for example, they are expressed to be for the benefit of adjoining land or are 'building scheme' covenants. If he purports to do so and subsequently conveys the unencumbered property as beneficial owner, he may be exposing himself to liabilities to his purchaser in the event of his purported release of the restrictive covenants being ineffective. For this reason, this clause contains an alternative. It is for the purchaser to decide whether he is legally capable of effecting the release; the Vendor has no part in it. It is unwise to purport to release the restrictive covenants if they are registered as D(ii) Land Charges because it may not be possible to remove the entry from the register. The Registrar contends (and rightly so it is submitted) that the owner of a rentcharge cannot release restrictive covenants that are expressed to be for the benefit of adjoining land unless he can also establish that he owns the entirety of the land intended to be benefited by those covenants.

Part 2 Leaseholds

67

Assignment of the whole of the property comprised in a lease[1]

This Assignment dated
is made between:
(1) the Vendor
(2) the Purchaser

1 The Vendor acknowledges the receipt from the Purchaser of £
the purchase price of the land and house known as [*postal address*] ('the
Property') which is fully described in a lease dated *etc* ('the Lease').

2 The Property is leasehold for a term of [999] years from [*date*] created
by the Lease.

3 The Vendor as beneficial owner assigns to the Purchaser the leasehold
estate in the Property.

4 The Property is subject to a yearly ground rent of £　　　made
payable by the Lease and to such covenants and restrictions contained
in the Lease as are still effective.

Add any appropriate standard clauses

Certificate of value (if applicable)

1   This precedent may be adapted for use in the case of an assignment of a short term lease at a rack rent. In that case, it is preferable that clause 4 should refer to 'rent' instead of 'ground rent'.

Where the assignment is for valuable consideration there will be covenants for the payment of rent, for the performance of the lesses covenants and for indemnity implied by LPA 1925, s 77(1)(C). In other cases, these covenants can be incorporated by the use of the following clause:

The same covenants shall be implied in this deed as if this assignment had been for valuable consideration.

68

Assignment of part of leasehold property by reference to an attached plan, the rent being apportioned[1]

This Assignment dated
is made between:
(1) the Vendor
(2) the Purchaser

1 The Vendor acknowledges the receipt from the Purchaser of £   the purchase price of the land and house known as [*postal address*] ('the Property Assigned') which is fully described in the first schedule.

2 The Property Assigned is leasehold for a term of [999] years from [*date*] created by a lease dated *etc* ('the Lease').

3 The Vendor as beneficial owner assigns to the Purchaser the leasehold estate in the Property Assigned.

4 (a) The Property Assigned and the land shown edged [blue] on the attached plan ('the Retained Premises') together comprise the whole of the property demised by the Lease and are subject to a yearly ground rent of £   made payable by the Lease.

(b) The Vendor and the Purchaser agree that from the date of this deed the yearly ground rent of £   is apportioned between the Property Assigned and the Retained Premises so that the Property Assigned is subject to a yearly ground rent of £   and the Retained Premises are subject to a yearly ground rent of £   .

5 The Vendor and the Purchaser declare that from the date of this deed:

(a) the Property Assigned stands charged with the payment of all money which may become payable under the covenants on the part of the Purchaser implied by the Law of Property Act 1925;[2]

(b) the Retained Premises stand charged with the payment of all money which may become payable under the covenants on the part of the Vendor implied by the Law of Property Act 1925;[2]

(c) any wall fence or hedge separating the Property Assigned from the Retained Premises shall be a party structure to be repaired and maintained at the equally shared expense of its owners;

(d) any sewers drains electricity cables gas pipes gutters downspouts and similar conduits serving both the Property Assigned and the

1   Please refer to the Appendix (pp 299ff) for observations of general application to sales-off and the apportionment of ground rents.

2   Strictly speaking this sub-clause could be omitted because clause 4 brings into operation LPA 1925, s 190.

Retained Premises shall continue to be used as they were prior to the date of this deed [and shall be repaired and maintained at the equally shared expense of the owners of the Property Assigned and of the Retained Premises];[3]

(e) no right of way over the Retained Premises shall be implied in this deed;[4]

(f) section 62 of the Law of Property Act 1925 shall not apply to this deed.[4]

6   The Property Assigned is subject to such covenants and restrictions contained in the Lease as are still effective and relate to it.

7   The Vendor undertakes to keep safe the documents listed in the second schedule and acknowledges the right of the Purchaser to their production and to the supply of copies.

Add any appropriate standard clauses

Certificate of value (if applicable)

First Schedule
The land and house known as [*postal address*] shown edged [red] on the attached plan.
There is excepted and reserved from this assignment any easement quasi-easement or right that prior to the date of this deed was enjoyed by the Vendor for the benefit of the Retained Premises and which continues to be necessary to the reasonable enjoyment of the Retained Premises.[5]

Second Schedule
List of documents to which the acknowledgment relates

3   Most draftsmen make provision for the cost of repairing and maintaining party structures to be borne by the parties in equal shares, as in the precedent. The cost of rebuilding, say, a party wall could be expensive. Moreover, neither party is likely to undertake the work without the other contributing to its cost. The same considerations do not apply to conduits. Some draftsmen prefer to make no provision for their maintenance, relying on the fact that the owner of each house is likely to undertake the repair of conduits on or under his own property and that, in many cases, it is hardly worth seeking a contribution. Different considerations would apply however to, say, a private sewer serving the two houses. In some circumstances, it may be proper to provide for the contribution to repairs to be in unequal shares. Whenever possible, however, it is preferable to define the contribution of the parties rather than make provision for the payment of a 'fair proportion of the cost' which can be a fruitful source of dispute in the future.

4   It is likely that this provision will require to be adapted to the circumstances. It has been inserted to remind the draftsman of the need to give consideration to these matters. See Appendix pp 299ff.

5   Please refer to the Appendix (pp 299ff) for observations concerning rights to be excepted.

69

Assignment of part of leasehold property, without reference to an attached plan the rent being apportioned[1]

This Assignment dated
is made between:
(1) the Vendor
(2) the Purchaser

1 The Vendor acknowledges the receipt from the Purchaser of
£   the purchase price of the land and house known as [*postal address*] ('the Property Assigned') which is fully described in the first schedule.

2 The Property Assigned is leasehold for a term of [999] from [*date*] created by a lease dated *etc* ('the Lease').

3 The Vendor as beneficial owner assigns to the Purchaser the leasehold estate in the Property Assigned.

4 (a) The Property Assigned and the remainder of the land demised by the Lease ('the Retained Premises') are together subject to a yearly ground rent of £   made payable by the Lease.

   (b) The Vendor and the Purchaser agree that from the date of this deed the yearly ground rent of £   is apportioned between the Property Assigned and the Retained Premises so that the Property Assigned is subject to a yearly ground rent of £   and the Retained Premises are subject to a yearly ground rent of £   .

5 The Vendor and the Purchaser declare that from the date of this deed:

   (a) the Property Assigned stands charged with the payment of all money which may become payable under the covenants on the part of the Purchaser implied by the Law of Property Act 1925;[2]

   (b) the Retained Premises stand charged with the payment of all money which may become payable under the covenants on the part of the Vendor implied by the Law of Property Act 1925;[2]

   (c) any wall fence or hedge separating the Property Assigned from the Retained Premises shall be a party structure to be repaired and maintained at the equally shared expense of its owners;

   (d) any sewers drains electricity cables gas pipes gutters downspouts or similar conduits serving both the Property Assigned and the Retained Premises shall continue to be used as they were prior to

170

1   Please refer to the Appendix (pp 299ff) for observations of general application to sales-off and the apportionment of ground rents.

2   Strictly speaking this sub-clause could be omitted because clause 4 brings into operation LPA 1925, s 190.

the date of this deed [and shall be repaired and maintained at the equally shared expense of the owners of the Property Assigned and of the Retained Premises];[3]

(e) no rights of way over the Retained Premises shall be implied in this deed;[4]

(f) section 62 of the Law of Property Act 1925 shall not apply to this deed.[4]

6 The Property Assigned is subject to such covenants and restrictions contained in the Lease as are still effective and relate to it.

7 The Vendor undertakes to keep safe the documents listed in the second schedule and acknowledges the right of the Purchaser to their production and to the supply of copies.

Add any appropriate standard clause

Certificate of value (if applicable)

First Schedule

The land and house known as [*postal address*] but except and reserved from this assignment any easement quasi-easement or right that prior to the date of this deed was enjoyed by the Vendor for the benefit of the Retained Premises and which continues to be necessary to the reasonable enjoyment of the Retained Premises.[5]

Second Schedule

List of documents to which the acknowledgment relates

3   Most draftsmen make provision for the cost of repairing and maintaining party structures to be borne by the parties in equal shares, as in the precedent. The cost of rebuilding, say, a party wall could be expensive. Moreover, neither party is likely to undertake the work without the other contributing to its cost. The same considerations do not apply to conduits. Some draftsmen prefer to make no provision for their maintenance, relying on the fact that the owner of each house is likely to undertake the repair of conduits on or under his own property and that, in many cases, it is hardly worth seeking a contribution. Different considerations would apply however to, say, a private sewer serving the two houses. In some circumstances, it may be proper to provide for the contribution to repairs to be in unequal shares. Whenever possible, however, it is preferable to define the contribution of the parties rather than make provision for the payment of a 'fair proportion of the cost' which can be a fruitful source of dispute in the future.

4   It is likely that this provision will require to be adapted to the circumstances. It has been inserted to remind the draftsman of the need to give consideration to these matters. See Appendix.

5   Please refer to the Appendix for observations concerning rights to be excepted.

70

Assignment of part of leasehold property where there has been a previous sale-off at an apportioned rent and there is a further apportionment on the present sale[1]

This Assignment dated
is made between:
(1) the Vendor
(2) the Purchaser

1 The Vendor acknowledges the receipt from the Purchaser of £ the purchase price of the land and house known as [*postal address*] ('the Property Assigned') which is fully described in the first schedule.

2 The Property Assigned is leasehold for a term of [999] years from [*date*] created by a lease dated *etc* ('the Lease').

3 The Vendor as beneficial owner assigns to the Purchaser the leasehold estate in the Property Assigned.

4 (a) The Property Assigned and the premises described in the second schedule ('the Retained Premises') are together subject to an apportioned yearly ground rent of £ which is part of the yearly ground rent of £ made payable by the Lease.

(b) The Vendor and the Purchaser agree that from the date of this deed the apportioned yearly ground rent £ is further apportioned so that the Property Assigned is subject to a yearly ground rent of £ and the Retained Premises are subject to a yearly ground rent of £ .

5 The Vendor and the Purchaser declare that from the date of this deed:

(a) the Property Assigned stands charged with the payment of all money which may become payable under the covenants on the part of the Purchaser implied by the Law of Property Act 1925;[2]

(b) the Retained Premises stand charged with the payment of all money which may become payable under the covenants on the part of the Vendor implied by the Law of Property Act 1925;[2]

(c) any wall fence or hedge separating the Property Assigned from the Retained Premises shall be a party structure to be repaired and maintained at the equally shared expense of its owners;

(d) any sewers drains electricity cables gas pipes gutters downspouts

174

1   Please refer to the Appendix (pp 299ff) for observations of general application to sales-off and the apportionment of ground rents.

2   Strictly speaking this sub-clause could be omitted because clause 4 brings into operation LPA 1925, s 190.

and similar conduits serving both the Property Assigned and the Retained Premises shall continue to be used as they were prior to the date of this deed [and shall be repaired and maintained at the equally shared expense of the owners of the Property Assigned and of the Retained Premises];[3]

(e) no right of way over the Retained Premises shall be implied in this deed;[4]

(f) section 62 of the Law of Property Act 1925 shall not apply to this deed.[4]

6   The Property Assigned is subject to:

(a) such covenants and restrictions contained in the Lease as are still effective and relate to the Property Assigned;

(b) the agreements declarations covenants and charges implied or contained in an assignment dated *etc* whereby part of the land demised by the Lease was assigned subject to an apportioned yearly ground rent of £   .

7   The Vendor undertakes to keep safe the documents listed in the third schedule and acknowledges the right of the Purchaser to their production and to the supply of copies.

Add any appropriate standard clauses

Certificate of value (if applicable)

First Schedule

The land and house known as [*postal address*] but except and reserved from this assignment any easement quasi-easement or right that prior to the date of this deed was enjoyed by the Vendor for the benefit of the Retained Premises and which continue to be necessary to the reasonable enjoyment of the Retained Premises.[5]

Second Schedule

The land and houses known as [*postal addresses of the Retained Premises*]

Third Schedule

List of documents to which the acknowledgment relates

3   Most draftsmen make provision for the cost of repairing and maintaining party structures to be borne by the parties in equal shares, as in the precedent. The cost of rebuilding, say, a party wall could be expensive. Moreover, neither party is likely to undertake the work without the other contributing to its cost. The same considerations do not apply to conduits. Some draftsmen prefer to make no provision for their maintenance, relying on the fact that the owner of each house is likely to undertake the repair of conduits on or under his own property and that, in many cases, it is hardly worth seeking a contribution. Different considerations would apply however to, say, a private sewer serving the two houses. In some circumstances, it may be proper to provide for the contribution to repairs to be in unequal shares. Whenever possible, however, it is preferable to define the contribution of the parties rather than make provision for the payment of a 'fair proportion of the cost' which can be a fruitful source of dispute in the future.

4   It is likely that this provision will require to be adapted to the circumstances. It has been inserted to remind the draftsman of the need to give consideration to these matters. See Appendix (pp 299ff).

5   Please refer to the Appendix for observations concerning rights to be excepted.

71

Assignment of part of leasehold property where there have been several previous sales-off at apportioned rents and there is a further apportionment on the present sale[1]

This Assignment dated
is made between:
(1) the Vendor
(2) the Purchaser

1 The Vendor acknowledges the receipt from the Purchaser of
£   the purchase price of the land and house known as [*postal address*] ('the Property Assigned') which is fully described in the first schedule.

2 The Property Assigned is leasehold for a term of [999] years from [*date*] created by a lease dated *etc* ('the Lease').

3 The Vendor as beneficial owner assigns to the Purchaser the leasehold estate in the Property Assigned.

4 (a) The Property Assigned and the premises described in the second schedule ('the Retained Premises') are together subject to an apportioned yearly ground rent of £   which is part of the yearly ground rent of £   made payable by the Lease.

    (b) The Vendor and the Purchaser agree that from the date of this deed the apportioned yearly ground rent of £   is further apportioned so that the Property Assigned is subject to a yearly ground rent of £   and the Retained Premises are subject to a yearly ground rent of £   .

5 The Vendor and the Purchase declare that from the date of this deed:

    (a) the Property Assigned stands charged with the payment of all money which may become payable under the covenants on the part of the Purchaser implied by the Law of Property Act 1925;[2]

    (b) the Retained Premises stand charged with the payment of all money which may become payable under the covenants on the part of the Vendor implied by the Law of Property Act 1925;[2]

    (c) any wall fence or hedge separating the Property Assigned from the Retained Premises shall be a party structure to be repaired and maintained at the equally shared expense of its owners;

    (d) any sewers drains electricity cables gas pipes gutters downspouts and similar conduits serving both the Property Assigned and the

178

1   Please refer to the Appendix (pp 299ff) for observations of general application to sales-off and the apportionment of ground rents.

2   Strictly speaking this sub-clause could be omitted because clause 4 brings into operation LPA 1925, s 190.

Retained Premises shall continue to be used as they were prior to the date of this deed [and shall be repaired and maintained at the equally shared expense of the owners of the Property Assigned and of the Retained Premises];[3]

(e) no right of way over the Retained Premises shall be implied in this deed;[4]

(f) section 62 of the Law of Property Act 1925 shall not apply to this deed.[4]

6   The Property Assigned is subject to:

(a) such covenants and restrictions contained in the Lease as are still effective and relate to the Property Assigned;

(b) the agreements declarations covenants and charges by each of the assignors implied or contained in the [four] assignments specified in the third schedule by which other houses comprised in the Lease have been sold off as set out in that schedule.

7   The Vendor undertakes to keep safe the documents listed in the fourth schedule and acknowledges the right of the Purchaser to their production and to the supply of copies.

Add any appropriate standard clauses

Certificate of value (if applicable)

First Schedule
Description of the Property Assigned[5]

Second Schedule
The land and houses known as [*postal addresses of the Retained Premises*]

Third Schedule

Date of Deed	Property Assigned	Parties	Apportioned rent

Fourth Schedule
List of documents to which the acknowledgment relates

3   Most draftsmen make provision for the cost of repairing and maintaining party structures to be borne by the parties in equal shares, as in the precedent. The cost of rebuilding, say, a party wall could be expensive. Moreover, neither party is likely to undertake the work without the other contributing to its cost. The same considerations do not apply to conduits. Some draftsmen prefer to make no provision for their maintenance, relying on the fact that the owner of each house is likely to undertake the repair of conduits on or under his own property and that, in many cases, it is hardly worth seeking a contribution. Different considerations would apply however to, say, a private sewer serving the two houses. In some circumstances, it may be proper to provide for the contribution to repairs to be in unequal shares. Whenever possible, however, it is preferable to define the contribution of the parties rather than make provision for the payment of a 'fair proportion of the cost' which can be a fruitful source of dispute in the future.

4   It is likely that this provision will require to be adapted to the circumstances. It has been inserted to remind the draftsman of the need to give consideration to these matters. See Appendix (pp 299ff).

5   Please refer to the first schedule to the preceding precedent and to the Appendix for observations concerning rights to be excepted.

72

Assignment of part of leasehold property where the rent has previously been apportioned to that part[1]

This Assignment dated
is made between:
(1) the Vendor
(2) the Purchaser

1 The Vendor acknowledges the receipt from the Purchaser of £   the purchase price of the land and house known as [*postal address*] ('the Property') which is fully described in an assignment dated *etc* ('the Assignment').

2 The Property is leasehold for a term of [999] years from [*date*] created by a lease dated *etc* ('the Lease').

3 The Vendor as beneficial owner assigns to the Purchaser the leasehold estate in the Property.

4 The Property is subject to:

(a) a yearly ground rent of £   made payable by the Assignment being an apportioned part of the yearly ground rent of £   reserved by the Lease;

(b) such covenants and restrictions contained in the Lease as are still effective and relate to the Property;

(c) the agreements declarations covenants and charges by [*the purchaser in the Assignment*] contained or implied in the Assignment.

Add any appropriate standard clauses

Certificate of value (if applicable)

1   Where the ground rent reserved by the original lease has been apportioned since 1925, the purchaser will take the property subject to and with the benefit of the covenants and charges relating to the apportionment contained or implied in the apportionment deed. See LPA 1925, ss 77(5) and 79. It is not strictly necessary therefore to include clause 4(c) but it is preferable that the deed should show the restrictions to which the property is subject although it is not so important that it should reveal that the purchaser has the statutory benefit of certain covenants.

Where the apportionment deed was before 1926 and contained express covenants similar to those now implied by LPA 1925, the property should be assigned subject to those covenants and the benefit of the covenants shall be expressly assigned to the purchaser. If LPA 1925, s 190 applied to the apportionment deed, no express assignment of the provisions of that section is necessary. See s 190(3).

Under LPA 1925, s 77 there will be implied covenants by the purchaser for the payment of the apportioned ground rent, for the performance of the lessees covenants and for indemnity. There are no corresponding implied covenants by the Vendor as he retains no part of the property demised by the Lease.

73

Assignment of residue of leasehold property, by reference to a plan, where other part previously sold off and rent apportioned

This Assignment dated
is made between:
(1) the Vendor
(2) the Purchaser

1 The Vendor acknowledges the receipt from the Purchaser of £   the purchase price of the land and house known as [*postal address*] ('the Property') which is fully described in the schedule.

2 The Property is leasehold for a term of [999] years from [*date*] created by a lease dated *etc* ('the Lease').

3 The Vendor as beneficial owner assigns to the Purchaser the leasehold estate in the Property.

4 The Property is subject to:

(a) an apportioned yearly ground rent of £   (part of the rent of £   reserved by the Lease) made payable by an assignment dated *etc* ('the Assignment') whereby the land shown edged [blue] on the attached plan (being part of the land demised by the lease) was assigned;

(b) such covenants and restrictions contained in the Lease as are still effective and relate to the Property;

(c) the agreements declarations covenants and charges by [*the vendor in the Assignment*] implied or contained in the Assignment.

Add any appropriate standard clauses

Certificate of value (if applicable)

Schedule
Description of the Property by reference to the attached plan.[1]

1   What rights are granted and excepted will be governed by the provisions of the earlier
sale-off. Perhaps a provision along the following lines would be suitable:
This assignment includes the rights expressed to be excepted from the Assignment
but there are excepted from this assignment the rights expressly or impliedly granted
by the Assignment that affect the Property.

74

Assignment of residue of leasehold property, without reference to a plan, where other part previously sold off and rent apportioned

This Assignment dated
is made between:
(1) the Vendor
(2) the Purchaser

1 The Vendor acknowledges the receipt from the Purchaser of £ the purchase price of the land and house known as [*postal address*] ('the Property') which is fully described in the schedule.

2 The Property is leasehold for a term of [999] years from [*date*] created by a lease dated *etc* ('the Lease').

3 The Vendor as beneficial owner assigns to the Purchaser the leasehold estate in the Property.

4 The Property is subject to:

(a) an apportioned yearly ground rent of £ (part of the rent of £ reserved by the Lease) made payable by an assignment dated *etc* ('the Assignment') whereby part of the land demised by the Lease was assigned;

(b) such covenants and restrictions contained in the Lease as are still effective and relate to the Property;

(c) the agreements declarations covenants and charges by [*the vendor in the Assignment*] implied or contained in the Assignment.

Add any appropriate standard clauses

Certificate of value (if applicable)

Schedule

The land demised by the Lease except such part as was assigned by the Assignment.[1]

1   What rights are granted and excepted will be governed by the provisions of the earlier
sale-off. Perhaps a provision along the following lines would be suitable:
    This assignment includes the rights expressed to be excepted from the Assignment
    but there are excepted from this assignment the rights expressly or impliedly granted
    by the Assignment that affect the Property.

75

Assignment of part of leasehold property the whole of the ground rent being charged on the land retained by the Vendor in exoneration of the property assigned

This Assignment dated
is made between:
(1) the Vendor
(2) the Purchaser

1 The Vendor acknowledges the receipt from the Purchaser of £ the purchase price of the land and house known as [*postal address*] ('the Property Assigned') which is fully described in the first schedule.

2 The Property Assigned is leasehold for [999] years from [*date*] created by a lease dated *etc* ('the Lease').

3 The Vendor as beneficial owner assigns to the Purchaser the leasehold estate in the Property Assigned.

If a plan is used

4 (a) The Property Assigned and the land shown edged [blue] on the attached plan ('the Retained Premises') together comprise the whole of the property demised by the Lease and are subject to the yearly ground rent of £ made payable by the Lease;

(b) The Vendor and the Purchaser agree that from the date of this deed the whole of the yearly ground rent of £ shall be charged on the Retained Premises in exoneration of the Property Assigned.

If a plan is not used

4 (a) The Property Assigned and the remainder of the land demised by the Lease ('the Retained Premises') are together subject to a yearly ground rent of £ made payable by the Lease.

(b) The Vendor and the Purchaser agree that from the date of this deed the whole of the yearly ground rent of £ shall be charged on the Retained Premises in exoneration of the Property Assigned.

5 The Property Assigned is subject to such covenants and restrictions contained in the Lease as are still effective and relate to it.

6   As a variant of the covenants referred to in section 77(1)(D) of the Law of Property Act 1925:[1]

   (a) the Vendor covenants with the Purchaser to pay the yearly ground rent of £   and to perform and observe such covenants and restrictions contained in the Lease as are still effective and relate to the Retained Premises and to indemnify the Vendor against any liability resulting from a breach of this covenant;

   (b) the Purchaser covenants with the Vendor to perform and observe such covenants and restrictions contained in the Lease as are still effective and relate to the Property Assigned and to indemnify the Purchaser against any liability resulting from a breach of this covenant.

7   The Vendor and the Purchaser declare that from the date of this deed:

   (a) the Property Assigned stands charged with the payment of all money which may become payable under the covenant on the part of the Purchaser contained in this deed;[2]

   (b) the Retained Premises stand charged with the payment of all money which may become payable under the covenant on the part of the Vendor contained in this deed;[2]

   (c) any wall fence or hedge separating the Property Assigned from the Retained Premises shall be a party structure to be repaired and maintained at the equally shared expense of its owners;[2]

   (d) any sewers drains electricity cables gas pipes gutters downspouts or similar conduits serving both the Property Assigned and the Retained Premises shall continue to be so used as they were prior to this date [and shall be repaired and maintained at the equally shared expense of the owners of the Property Assigned and of the Retained Premises];[3]

   (e) no right of way over the Retained Premises shall be implied in this deed;[4]

   (f) section 62 of the Law of Property Act 1925 shall not apply to this deed.[4]

8   The Vendor undertakes to keep safe the documents listed in the second schedule and acknowledges the right of the Purchaser to their production and to the supply of copies.

Add any appropriate standard clauses

Certificate of value (if applicable)

1   LPA 1925, s 77(2) is obscure but it appears that a covenant is implied on the part of the vendor for payment of the entire ground rent, for the performance of the covenants and restrictions relating to the retained property and for indemnity. It is not clear from that section, however, that any covenant is implied on the part of the purchaser for the performance of the covenants and restrictions affecting the property conveyed. Conveyancers are not agreed upon whether a covenant is implied or not and the general practice is to insert an express convenant by the purchaser. This practice has been followed here. An express covenant by the vendor has also been included, partly because of the purchaser's express covenant and partly because of the inept wording of s 77(2). Both covenants are expressed to be variants of the covenants referred to in s 77(1)(D) so as to obtain the benefit of the provisions of s 77(6) by virtue of s 77(4).

Please refer to the Appendix for observations of general application to sales-off.

2   Strictly speaking this sub-clause could be omitted because clause 4 brings into operation LPA 1925, s 190.

3   Most draftsmen make provision for the cost of repairing and maintaining party structures to be borne by the parties in equal shares, as in the precedent. The cost of rebuilding, say, a party wall could be expensive. Moreover, neither party is likely to undertake the work without the other contributing to its cost. The same considerations do not apply to conduits. Some draftsmen prefer to make no provision for their maintenance, relying on the fact that the owner of each house is likely to undertake the repair of conduits on or under his own property and that, in many cases, it is hardly worth seeking a contribution. Different considerations would apply however to, say, a private sewer serving the two houses. In some circumstances, it may be proper to provide for the contribution to repairs to be in unequal shares. Whenever possible, however, it is preferable to define the contribution of the parties rather than make provision for the payment of a 'fair proportion of the cost' which can be a fruitful source of dispute in the future.

4   It is likely that this provision requires to be adapted to the circumstances. It has been inserted to remind the draftsman of the need to give consideration to these matters. See Appendix.

First Schedule

The land and house known as [*postal address*] shown edged red on the attached plan] *etc.*

There is excepted from this assignment any easement quasi-easement or right that prior to the date of this deed was enjoyed by the Vendor for the benefit of the Retained Premises and which continue to be necessary to the reasonable enjoyment of the Retained Premises.[5]

Second Schedule

List of documents to which the acknowledgment relates

5   Please refer to the Appendix (pp 299ff) for observations concerning rights to be excepted.

76

Assignment of part of leasehold property charged with the whole of the ground rent in exoneration of the land retained by the Vendor

This Assignment dated
is made between:
(1) the Vendor
(2) the Purchaser

1 The Vendor acknowledges the receipt from the Purchaser of £   the purchase price of the land and house known as [*postal address*] ('the Property Assigned') which is fully described in the first schedule.

2 The Property Assigned is leasehold for [999] years from [*date*] created by a lease dated *etc* ('the Lease').

3 The Vendor as beneficial owner assigns to the Purchaser the leasehold estate in the Property Assigned.

4 (a) The Property Assigned and the land shown edged [blue] on the attached plan ('the Retained Premises') together comprise the whole of the property demised by the Lease and are subject to the yearly ground rent of £   made payable by the Lease.

    (b) The Vendor and the Purchaser agree that from the date of this deed the whole of the ground rent of £   shall be charged on the Property Assigned in exoneration of the Retained Premises.

or where there is no plan

4 (a) The Property Assigned and the remainder of the land demised by the Lease ('the Retained Premises') are together subject to a yearly ground rent of £   made payable by the Lease.

    (b) The Vendor and the Purchaser agree that from the date of this deed the whole of the yearly ground rent of £   shall be charged on the Property Assigned in exoneration of the Retained Premises.

5 The Property Assigned is subject to such covenants and restrictions contained in the Lease as are still effective and relate to it.

6 As a variant of the covenants referred to in section 77(1)(D) of the Law of Property Act 1925:[1]

    (a) the Purchaser covenants with the Vendor to pay the yearly ground rent of £   and to perform and observe such

1 See note 1 to preceding precedent. Here the converse is the case. It is fairly clear that a covenant is implied on the part of the purchaser but it is not clear that any covenant is implied on the part of the vendor.

covenants and restrictions contained in the Lease as are still effective and relate to the Property Assigned and to indemnify the Vendor against any liability resulting from a breach of this covenant;

(b) the Vendor covenants with the Purchaser to perform and observe such covenants and restrictions contained in the Lease as are still effective and relate to the Retained Premises and to indemnify the Purchaser against any liability resulting from a breach of this covenant.

7   The Vendor and the Purchaser declare that from the date of this deed:

(a) the Property Assigned stands charged with the payment of all money which may become payable under the covenant on the part of the Purchaser contained in this deed;[2]

(b) the Retained Premises stand charged with the payment of all money which may become payable under the covenant on the part of the Vendor contained in this deed;[2]

(c) any wall fence or hedge separating the Property Assigned from the Retained Premises shall be a party structure to be repaired and maintained at the equally shared expense of its owners;

(d) any sewers drains electricity cables gas pipes gutters downspouts and similar conduits serving both the Property Assigned and the Retained Premises shall continue to be used as they were prior to the date of this deed [and shall be repaired and maintained at the equally shared expense of the owners of the Property Conveyed and of the Retained Premises];[3]

(e) no right of way over the Retained Premises shall be implied in this assignment;[4]

(f) section 62 of the Law of Property Act 1925 shall not apply to this deed.[4]

8   The Vendor undertakes to keep safe the documents listed in the second schedule and acknowledges the right of the Purchaser to their production and to the supply of copies.

Add any appropriate standard clauses

Certificate of value (if applicable)

First Schedule

The land and house known as [*postal address*] [shown edged red on the attached plan]

There is excepted from this Assignment any easement quasi-easement

2 Strictly speaking this sub-clause could be omitted because clause 4 bring into operation LPA 1925, s 190.

3 Most draftsmen make provision for the cost of repairing and maintaining party structures to be borne by the parties in equal shares, as in the precedent. The cost of rebuilding, say, a party wall could be expensive. Moreover, neither party is likely to undertake the work without the other contributing to its cost. The same considerations do not apply to conduits. Some draftsmen prefer to make no provision for their maintenance, relying on the fact that the owner of each house is likely to undertake the repair of conduits on or under his own property and that, in many cases, it is hardly worth seeking a contribution. Different considerations would apply however to, say, a private sewer serving the two houses. In some circumstances, it may be proper to provide for the contribution to repairs to be in unequal shares. Whenever possible, however, it is preferable to define the contribution of the parties rather than make provision for the payment of a 'fair proportion of the cost' which can be a fruitful source of dispute in the future.

4 It is likely that this provision requires to be adapted to the circumstances. It has been inserted to remind the draftsman of the need to give consideration to these matters. See Appendix (pp 299ff).

or right that prior to the date of this deed was enjoyed by the vendor for the benefit of the Retained Premises and which continues to be necessary to the reasonable enjoyment of the Retained Premises.[5]

Second Schedule
List of documents to which the acknowledgment relates

5   Please refer to the Appendix for observations concerning rights to be excepted.

77

Assignment of property comprised in a lease subject to but with the benefit of underleases constituting previous sales-off[1]

This Assignment dated
is made between:
(1) the Vendor
(2) the Purchaser

1 The Vendor acknowledges the receipt from the Purchaser of £   the purchase price of the land and houses known as [*postal address*] ('the Property') which is fully described in a lease dated *etc* ('the Lease').

2 The Property is leasehold for a term of [999] years from [*date*] created by the Lease.

3 The Vendor as beneficial owner assigns to the Purchaser the leasehold estate in the Property and also the benefit of the ground rents created by the [five] underleases specified in the schedule ('the Underleases') together with all powers and remedies securing their payment and the benefit of the covenants and restrictions contained in the Underleases.

4 The Property is subject to:

(a) the yearly ground rent of £   made payable by the Lease;

(b) such of the covenants and restrictions contained in the Lease as are still effective;

(c) the terms of years created by the Underleases and the lessors covenants contained in the Underleases;

(d) the agreements and declarations and the provisions relating to common easements in the Underleases [numbered in the schedule].[2]

Add any appropriate standard clauses

Certificate of value (if applicable)

Schedule

Number	Address of property	Date of Underlease	Parties	Term	Rent

1   To the layman this is an assignment of the residue of the property comprised in the lease together with the right to receive the ground rents reserved by the underleases. In law, of course, it is an assignment of the whole of the property demised by the lease subject to but with the benefit of the underleases.

2   This is intended to provide for the situation where one or more of earlier sales-off have contained agreements and declarations relating to party structures and common easements.

78

Assignment of leasehold reversion[1]

This Assignment dated
is made between:
(1) the Vendor
(2) the Purchaser

1 The Vendor acknowledges the receipt from the Purchaser of
£   the purchase price of the leasehold reversion in the land
and houses known as [*postal address*] ('the Property') which is described
in a lease dated *etc* ('the Lease').

2 The Property is leasehold for a term of [999] from [*date*] created by
the Lease.

3 The Vendor as beneficial owner assigns to the Purchaser the leasehold
estate in the Property subject to an underlease dated *etc* ('the Underlease')
but with the benefit of the ground rent created by the Underlease together
with all powers and remedies securing its payment and the benefit of the
covenants and restrictions contained in the Underlease.

4 The Property is subject to the yearly ground rent of £
made payable by the Lease and to such covenants and restrictions
contained in the Lease as are still effective.

Add any appropriate standard clauses

Certificate of value (if applicable)

1   If the assignment is in favour of the owner of the Underlease, provision should be made for the merger or non-merger of the two estates and one of the following clauses inserted after clause 4

The Purchaser as the owner of the leasehold estates created by both the Lease and the Underlease declares that from the date of this deed the Underlease shall no longer continue in force but shall be merged in the leasehold estate created by the Lease.

or

The Purchaser declares that notwithstanding that he is now the owner of the leasehold estates created by both the Underlease and the Lease the Underlease shall continue in force and shall not merge in the leasehold estate created by the Lease.

See note 1 to precedent 15 for the rules relating to merger generally. The assignment of a leasehold reversion is relatively uncommon. If several underleases have been created out of the leasehold estate created by the head lease, this precedent can be adapted by reference to precedent 16.

79

Assignment of leasehold property to freehold reversioner—provision for merger or non-merger

This Assignment dated
is made between:
(1) the Vendor
(2) the Purchaser

1 The Vendor acknowledges the receipt from the Purchaser of £ the purchase price of the land and house known as [*postal address*] ('the Property') which is described in a lease dated *etc* ('the Lease').

2 The Property is leasehold for a term of [999] years from [*date*] created by the Lease.

3 The Vendor as beneficial owner assigns to the Purchaser the leasehold estate in the Property.

4 The Purchaser as the owner of the fee simple estate and of the leasehold estate in the Property declares that from the date of this deed the Lease shall no longer continue in force but shall be merged in the fee simple.

or

4 The Purchaser declares that notwithstanding that he is now the owner of the fee simple estate and of the leasehold estate in the Property the Lease shall continue in force and shall not merge with the fee simple.

5   Add any appropriate standard clauses

6   Certificate of value (if applicable)

Part 3 Mortgages vacating receipts and property subject to mortgages

80

Mortgage repayable on notice[1]

This Mortgage dated
is made between:
(1) the Borrower
(2) the Lender

1   In this deed:

(a) 'the Loan' means the sum of £   .

(b) 'the Mortgage Money' means the Loan and all other money
which may be owing to the Lender under this deed.[2]

2   The Borrower acknowledges the receipt of the Loan from the Lender.

3   The Borrower as beneficial owner charges the property described in
the first schedule ('the Property') by way of legal mortgage with the
payment of the Mortgage Money.

4   (a) If the Lender gives to the Borrower [three] months' written notice
requiring repayment of the Mortgage Money then on the expiry
of the notice the Borrower shall pay the Mortgage Money to the
Lender with interest to the date of payment [but the Lender shall
not be entitled to give notice requiring repayment before [date]
so long as the Borrower complies with his obligations under this
deed].

(b) The Borrower may redeem this Mortgage [after   ]:[3]
    (i) by giving to the Lender [three] months' written notice of his
    intention to do so and on the expiry of the notice paying to
    the Lender the Mortgage Money with interest to the date of
    redemption; or
    (ii) by paying to the Lender the Mortgage Money with interest
    to the date of redemption and three months' interest in lieu
    of notice.

5   (a) The Borrower shall pay interest on the Mortgage Money
(calculated with half yearly rests) on [date] and [date] in every
year at the annual rate of [per cent] or [
per cent above the base rate of   Bank plc in force on
the date when interest is payable].[4]

(b) The Lender may require payments of interest to be by direct
debit and the Borrower shall then take all necessary steps to give
effect to that requirement.

208

1   This precedent can easily be adapted to a mortgage repayable on demand by substituting the following as clause 4:

> The Borrower shall pay the Mortgage money to the Lender on demand.

2   The advantages of defining 'the Mortgage Money' in this way are:
   (a) There is then no need to keep referring in the body of the deed to 'the Loan and all other moneys secured by this deed' because the Property is security for the Mortgage Money and not merely for the Loan;
   (b) There is no necessity to make provision for payments made under clause 7 of the deed to attract interest and to be added to the Loan if not refunded by the borrower. Clause 7(d) is only included to cover the unlikely event of the Borrower tendering redemption money before the money expended by the lender has been demanded.
   (c) If interest is not paid on the due date it will constitute 'money owing to the Lender', become part of the Mortgage Money and itself attract interest.

3   The need to postpone the right to redeem is not likely to arise in the kind of mortgage for which this precedent is designed. If the right to redeem is postponed, care should be taken that it does not constitute a clog on the equity rendering it unenforceable.

4   The fluctuation in the rates of interest make fixed rate interest unattractive and the use of a rate of interest referable to bank base rate will be more usual. The wording here uses as the reference point the base rate operative on the date on which a particular payment of interest is due. The careful draftsman may wish to provide against a change of rate occurring on an interest date by adding '(or the higher rate if there is a change of base rate on that date)'.

Alternatively, the rate could be calculated on a day to day basis in which case, the following clause is suggested:

> The Borrower shall pay interest on the Mortgage Money on [*date*] and [*date*] in every year accruing from day to day at the rate of   % above the base rate of Bank plc

6   The Borrower covenants with the Lender in the terms of the second schedule.

7   (a) If the Borrower does not perform his covenant relating to insurance the Lender may insure the Property on such terms as he thinks fit.

(b) The Lender may enter the Property to remedy any breach of the Borrowers covenants but by doing so shall not become a mortgagee in possession.

(c) The Lender may discharge any financial obligation of the Borrower relating to the Property.

(d) Any money expended by the Lender under this clause shall be a charge on the Property even if the Lender has not demanded its payment by the Borrower.

8   The Lenders power of sale and other statutory powers shall arise on the date of this deed.[5]

9   The Mortgage Money shall become immediately payable and the Lender may exercise his statutory powers without giving notice to the Borrower:[6]

(a) if any interest has not been paid in full within [one month] of its becoming due; or

(b) if the Borrower is in breach of any of the provisions of this deed.

10   The Borrower shall not have the rights of leasing the Property granted by section 99 of the Law of Property Act 1925.

11   The restriction on the Lenders right of consolidation contained in section 93 of the Law of Property Act 1925 shall not apply.[7]

First Schedule

Description of Property

Second Schedule[8]

Borrowers covenants

1   To pay on demand any money spent by the Lenders exercising the powers in clause 7 or enforcing his other rights under this deed.

2   To keep the property insured[9] for its full reinstatement value against the risks normally covered by [a householder's comprehensive policy] in accordance with the following provisions:

(a) the insurers [and the agency for the insurance] shall be nominated [*or* approved] by the Lender;

(b) the Lender's interest shall be indorsed on the policy;

5   A purchaser from a lender who realises his security must ascertain that the power of sale has arisen but not whether the power has become exercisable. The power to sell, to foreclose and to appoint a receiver arises 'when the mortgage money has become due'. The traditional way of bringing the statutory provision into operation has been to provide for repayment of the loan on a date three or six months after the date of the deed. This is an artificial device because neither the lender nor the borrower intend that repayment shall take place at that time. LPA 1925, s 101(3) provides that the statutory powers of a lender may be varied or extended by the mortgage deed and clause 8 ensures that the lender has the power of sale etc from the outset.

6   LPA 1925, s 103 places restrictions on the exercise of the power of sale by a lender and this clause reduces the scope of those restrictions.

7   In many cases this clause will not be required.

8   These are suggested covenants and will require to be adapted to the circumstances.

9   The lender may prefer to effect the insurance himself and recover the premium from the borrower. In this event clause 7(a) of the deed should be changed to read:

The Lender shall keep the Property insured against the risks normally covered by [a householder's comprehensive policy] and otherwise as he sees fit.

The reimbursement of the premiums will be covered by covenant 1 but it is desirable that there be substituted for covenant 2 the following:

Not to effect any insurance against risks covered by the policy effected by the Lender under clause 7.

This will prevent double insurance and the problems that can ensue from it. The suggested substitution for clause 7(a) places an obligation on the lender to effect the insurance. He may not be prepared to assume this responsibility and prefer 'may' to 'shall' in clause 7(a). This highlights the problem of insurance. Whichever party is to insure, the other wishes to be certain that the insurance is in force. If the Lender has an agency with an insurance company, probably the best solution is for the borrower to insure through that agency as this enables the lender to monitor the cover and the payment of premiums.

(c) on request the Borrower shall produce the policy to the Lender and furnish evidence that the policy is in force;

(d) no other insurance against the same risks shall be effected by the Borrower.

3   To keep the Property in repair[10] and to permit the Lender to inspect its state of repair.

4   To perform and observe any covenants and restrictions relating to the Property.

5   (a) Not without the Lender's permission to carry out any development within the meaning of the Town and Country Planning legislation.

(b) Not to contravene any of the provisions of Town and Country Planning legislation.

(c) Within 7 days of receiving any document relating to planning or any other matter which might affect the Lender's security to give particulars to the Lender.

6   Not without the Lender's consent to make any alterations or additions to the Property.

7   Not to let or agree to let the Property or any part of it but to occupy it personally [as a residence for the Borrower and his family].

8   Not to sell or in any other way dispose of his interest in the Property.

9   Not to allow any person to be registered as proprietor of the Property under the Land Registration Act 1925.

10   Not to create a further charge on the Property.

11   To keep the Property free from any charge by the local authority.

10   There is no need to qualify the obligation to repair by adjectives or adverbs such as 'good' or 'substantially'.

81

Mortgage repayable by instalments with interest in addition

This Mortgage dated
is made between:
(1) the Borrower
(2) the Lender

1 In this deed:

(a) 'the Loan' means the sum of £   .

(b) 'the Mortgage Money' means the outstanding balance of the Loan and all other money which may be owing to the Lender under this deed.[1]

2 The Borrower acknowledges the receipt of the Loan from the Lender.

3 The Borrower as beneficial owner charges the property described in the first schedule ('the Property') by way of legal mortgage with the payment of the Mortgage Money.

4 (a) The Borrower shall repay the Loan by [monthly] instalments of £   starting on [*date of first payment*] to be made by direct debit [*or* bankers standing order]

(b) On paying any instalment the Borrower may make an additional payment [of not less than £   ].

5 The Borrower shall pay interest on the Mortgage Money (calculated with half yearly rests) on [*date*] and [*date*] in every year at the annual rate of [per cent] *or* [per cent above the base rate of   Bank plc in force on the date when interest is payable].[2]

6 The Borrower covenants with the Lender in the terms of the second schedule.

7 (a) If the Borrower does not perform his covenant relating to insurance the Lender may insure the Property on such terms as he thinks fit.

(b) The Lender may enter the Property to remedy any breach of the Borrowers covenants but by doing so shall not become a mortgagee in possession.

(c) The Lender may discharge any financial obligation of the Borrower relating to the Property.

(d) Any money expended by the Lender under this clause shall be a charge on the Property even if the Lender has not demanded its payment by the Borrower.

1   The advantages of defining 'the Mortgage Money' in this way are:
   (a) There is then no need to keep referring in the body of the deed to 'the Loan and all other moneys secured by this deed' because the Property is security for the Mortgage Money and not merely for the Loan;
   (b) There is no necessity to make provision for payments made under clause 7 of the deed to attract interest and to be added to the Loan if not refunded by the borrower. Clause 7(d) is only included to cover the unlikely event of the Borrower tendering redemption money before the money expended by the lender has been demanded.
   (c) If interest is not paid on the due date it will constitute 'money owing to the Lender', become part of the Mortgage Money and itself attract interest.

2   The fluctuation in the rates of interest make fixed rate interest unattractive and the use of a rate of interest referable to bank base rate will be more usual. The wording here uses as the reference point the base rate operative on the date on which a particular payment of interest is due. The careful draftsman may wish to provide against a change of rate occurring on an interest date by adding '(or the higher rate if there is a change of base rate on that date'.)
Alternatively, the rate could be calculated on a day to day basis in which case, the following clause is suggested:
   The Borrower shall pay interest on the Mortgage Money on [*date*] and [*date*] in every year accruing from day to day at the rate of   % above the base rate of
   Bank plc

8   The Lenders power of sale and other statutory powers shall arise on the date of this deed.[3]

9   The Mortgage Money shall become immediately payable and the Lender may exercise his statutory powers without giving notice to the Borrower:[4]

   (a) If the Borrower is in arrear with the [monthly] instalments to the extent of £   ; or

   (b) If any interest has not been paid in full within one month of its becoming due; or

   (c) If the Borrower is in breach of any of the provisions of this deed.

10   The Borrower shall not have the rights of leasing the Property granted by section 99 of the Law of Property Act 1925.

11   The restriction on the Lenders right of consolidation contained in section 93 of the Law of Property Act 1925 shall not apply.[5]

First Schedule

Description of Property

Second Schedule

Borrowers covenants
See second schedule to precedent 80.
It is desirable to incorporate the additional covenant set out below which, it is suggested, should be covenant number 2:

   After repayment of the Loan to continue to pay the [monthly] instalments until the whole of the Mortgage Money has been paid.

3   A purchaser from a lender who realises his security must ascertain that the power of sale has arisen but not whether the power has become exercisable. The power to sell, to foreclose and to appoint a receiver arise 'when the mortgage money has become due'. The traditional way of bringing the statutory provision into operation has been to provide for repayment of the loan on a date three or six months after the date of the deed. This is an artificial device because neither the lender nor the borrower intend that repayment shall take place at that time. LPA 1925, s 101(3) provides that the statutory powers of a lender may be varied or extended by the mortgage deed and clause 8 ensures that the lender has the power of sale etc from the outset.

4   LPA 1925, s 103 places restrictions on the exercise of the power of sale by a lender and this clause reduces the scope of those restrictions.

5   In many cases this clause will not be required.

82

Mortgage with capital and interest repayable after the style of a building society mortgage

This Mortgage dated
is made between:
(1) the Borrower
(2) the Lender

1   In this deed:

   (a) 'the Loan' means the sum of £   .

   (b) 'the Mortgage Money' means the outstanding balance of the Loan and all other money which may be owing to the Lender under this deed.[1]

2   The Borrower acknowledges the receipt of the Loan from the Lender.

3   The Borrower as beneficial owner charges the property described in the first schedule ('the Property') by way of legal mortgage with the payment of the Mortgage Money.

4   (a) The Borrower shall pay the Mortgage Money by [monthly] instalments of £   starting on [date] to be made by direct debit [or bankers standing order].

   (b) On paying any instalment the Borrower may make an additional payment [of not less than £   ].

   (c) All payments by the Borrower shall be applied in accordance with the provisions of the second schedule.

   (d) The computation provided for in the second schedule shall be set out in a written statement sent by the Lender to the Borrower within [one] month of the end of each period of [six months] and if the Borrower does not make any objection to the statement within [fourteen] days of receiving it then it shall constitute an agreed statement of the Mortgage Money due to the Lender at the beginning of the next period of [six months] and shall be binding on both parties except for any obvious mistake.

5   There shall be added to the Mortgage Money on [date] and [date] in each year interest on the Mortgage Money (calculated with half yearly rests) at the annual rate of [per cent] or [per cent above the base rate of   Bank plc in force on the date when the interest becomes due].[2]

6   The Borrower covenants with the Lender in the terms of the third schedule.

1 The advantages of defining 'the Mortgage Money' in this way are:

  (a) There is then no need to keep referring in the body of the deed to 'the Loan and all other moneys secured by this deed' because the Property is security for the Mortgage Money and not merely for the Loan;

  (b) There is no necessity to make provision for payments made under clause 7 of the deed to attract interest and to be added to the Loan if not refunded by the borrower. Clause 7(d) is only included to cover the unlikely event of the Borrower tendering redemption money before the money expended by the lender has been demanded.

  (c) If interest is not paid on the due date it will constitute 'money owing to the Lender', become part of the Mortgage Money and itself attract interest.

2 The fluctuation in the rates of interest make fixed rate interest unattractive and the use of a rate of interest referable to bank base rate will be more usual. The wording here uses as the reference point the base rate operative on the date on which a particular payment of interest is due. The careful draftsman may wish to provide against a change of rate occurring on an interest date by adding '(or the higher rate if there is a change of base rate on that date)'.

Alternatively, the rate could be calculated on a day to day basis in which case, the following clause is suggested:

> The Borrower shall pay interest on the Mortgage Money on [*date*] and [*date*] in every year accruing from day to day at the rate of   % above the base rate of   Bank plc

7 (a) If the Borrower does not perform his covenant relating to insurance the Lender may insure the Property on such terms as he thinks fit.

(b) The Lender may enter the Property to remedy any breach of the Borrowers covenants but by doing so shall not become a mortgagee in possession.

(c) The Lender may discharge any financial objection of the Borrower relating to the Property.

(d) Any money expended by the Lender under this clause shall be a charge on the Property even if the Lender has not demanded its payment by the Borrower.

8 The Lenders power of sale and other statutory powers shall arise on the date of this deed.[3]

9 The Mortgage Money shall become immediately payable and the Lender may exercise his power of sale and other statutory powers without giving notice to the Borrower:[4]

(a) If the Borrower is in arrear with the [monthly] instalments to the extent of £   ; or

(b) If the Borrower is in breach of any of the provisions of this deed.

10 The Borrower shall not have the rights of leasing the Property granted by section 99 of the Law of Property Act 1925.

11 The restriction on the Lenders right of consolidation contained in section 93 of the Law of Property Act 1925 shall not apply.[5]

First Schedule

Description of Property

Second Schedule

1 At the end of a period of [six months] from [the date of this deed] there shall be added to the Mortgage Money the interest on the Mortgage Money for the [six month] period.

2 From this total there shall be deducted the payments made by the Borrower during the [six month] period.

3 The resulting figure shall constitute the Mortgage Money at the beginning of the next period of [six months].

4 At the end of each succeeding period of [six months] a similar calculation shall be made until the whole of the Mortgage Money has been paid.

Third Schedule

Borrower's covenants
See second schedule to precedent 80.

3   A purchaser from a lender who realises his security must ascertain that the power of sale has arisen but not whether the power has become exercisable. The power to sell, to foreclose and to appoint a receiver arise 'when the mortgage money has become due'. The traditional way of bringing the statutory provision into operation has been to provide for repayment of the loan on a date three or six months after the date of the deed. This is an artifical device because neither the lender nor the borrower intend that repayment shall take place at that time. LPA 1925, s 101(3) provides that the statutory powers of a lender may be varied or extended by the mortgage deed and clause 8 ensures that the lender has the power of sale etc from the outset.

4   LPA 1925, s 103 places restrictions on the exercise of the power of sale by a lender and this clause reduces the scope of those restrictions.

5   In many cases this clause will not be required.

83

Memorandum of Deposit[1]

This Memorandum of Deposit dated
is made between:
(1) the Borrower
(2) the Lender

1 The Borrower acknowledges the receipt of a loan of £
('the Loan') from the Lender.

2 Until repayment the Borrower will pay to the Lender interest on the
Loan [half yearly] on   and   at the annual rate of
[per cent] *or* [per cent above the base rate
of   Bank plc in force from time to time].

3 As security the Borrower has deposited with the Lender the documents
of title relating to [*postal address or short description of the security*].

1   The disadvantage of a memorandum of deposit under hand only is that the lender can do nothing to enforce the security except by court order. A memorandum of deposit under seal is, therefore, to be preferred. See next precedent.

84

Memorandum of Deposit under seal[1]

This Memorandum of Deposit dated
is made between:
(1) the Borrower
(2) the Lender

1   The Borrower acknowledges the receipt of a loan of £
('the Loan') from the Lender.

2   Until repayment the Borrower will pay to the Lender interest on the
Loan [half yearly] on   and   at the annual rate of [
per cent] *or* [per cent above the base rate of   Bank plc in
force from time to time].

3   As security the Borrower has deposited with the Lender the documents
of title relating to [*postal address or short description of the security*] ('the
Property').

4   When required by the Lender the Borrower will execute a legal
charge of the Property in favour of the Lender securing all money owing
under this deed and containing such provisions as are reasonably
required by the Lender and in the meantime the Borrower will hold the
Property on trust for the Lender who may at any time during the
continuance of this security appoint another person (including himself)
as a trustee in place of the Borrower.

5   The Lender shall have the right to take possession of the Property at
any time.

and/or the rents and profits thereof

SIGNED SEALED & DELIVERED by the said G — C — H — as a Deed in the presence of:—

1   All the ordinary powers and remedies of a mortgage under LPA 1925, s 101 are available to the lender where the memorandum of deposit is under seal.

85

Mortgage of a beneficial interest in freehold or leasehold property[1]

This Mortgage dated
is made between:
(1) the Borrower
(2) the Lender

1 The Borrower acknowledges the receipt from the Lender of a loan of £   ('the Loan').

2 Until repayment the Borrower shall pay interest on the Loan on [*date*] and [*date*] in every year calculated from day to day at the rate of   % above the base rate of   Bank plc.[2]

3 The Borrower shall repay the Loan on demand.

4 The Borrower as beneficial owner charges his [half] share in the proceeds of sale of the property described in the first schedule ('the Property') with the repayment of the Loan and all other money due to the Lender under this deed.

5 The Borrower covenants with the Lender that:

(a) he will perform and observe such of the covenants set out in the second schedule as are capable of performance and observance by him personally;

(b) he will ensure that the remaining covenants are performed and observed by others.[3]

6 The Lender's power of sale and other statutory powers shall arise on the date of this deed.

First Schedule

Description of Property

Second Schedule

See second schedule to Precedent 80.
Some adaptation may be required, for example, the detail of covenant 2 may have to be omitted; covenant 7 may not be appropriate; covenant 10 may have to be varied.

1   A beneficial share in property is, of course, rather unsatisfactory security. Often it is given as additional security, as security for a temporary loan, or as security for a loan not based on commercial considerations. In these circumstances, the mortgage is a long stop security and it may not be necessary to include the fairly detailed provisions of this precedent. Even in this fairly detailed precedent it has not been thought necessary to include clauses 9, 10 and 11 from precedent 80.

Notice of the mortgage should be given to the trustees of the property. If the borrower is a beneficial joint tenant, this mortgage will operate to sever the beneficial joint tenancy.

As the interest charged is equitable, the mortgage is necessarily equitable. As the document is under seal it is within the statutory definition of the mortgage contained in LPA 1925, s 205(1)(xvi) and the lender will therefore be in the same position as an equitable mortgagee as regards sale or the appointment of a receiver without resort to a court order.

2   See note 5 to precedent 80.

3   Covenants to repair, insure etc are included because the state of the property obviously affects the value of the security and, in the event of default, the power of sale could become exercisable. It is immaterial to the lender whether the covenants are performed by the borrower personally or by those in whom the legal estate is vested. Indeed, from the lender's point of view, it would be sufficient for the borrower to covenant to perform the covenants in the second schedule but it is illogical to require the borrower to perform covenants that he is not capable of performing personally.

86

Transfer of mortgage[1]

This Transfer of Mortgage dated
is made between:
(1) the Lender
(2) the Transferee

1 This deed is supplemental to a mortgage dated *etc* ('the Mortgage').

2 The Lender acknowledges the receipt from the Transferee of
£   .

3 The Lender as beneficial owner assigns to the Transferee the benefit of the Mortgage.

4 The Lender warrants that all interest under the Mortgage has been paid to date and the outstanding principal is £   .[2]

1   It is comparatively unusual for the borrower to join in a transfer of mortgage. There are a number of reasons for this. First, it is not necessary. Secondly, the borrower may be unwilling to join in the deed (and he cannot be compelled to do so) and, thirdly, the lender and transferee may not wish the borrower to be privy to the terms of the transfer if, for example, the transferee has paid less than the balance of the principal then owed. Obviously, if the borrower is not a party, he must be given notice of the transfer.

LPA 1925, s 114 governs the transfer of mortgages and, in effect, puts the transferee in the same position as he would have been in if he had been the original lender.

In precedent 87 the borrower is a party and by executing the transfer admits the amount outstanding under the mortgage. If the borrower is not a party to the transfer, the transferee will get only the benefit of the sum actually due even if the lender has represented that more is owing.

No Stamp Duty is payable on a transfer of mortgage.

2   This will enable the transferee to sue the lender in the event of the balance due under the mortgage being over-stated. A warranty is to be preferred to a covenant by the lender.

87

Transfer of mortgage—the mortgagor joining in[1]

This Transfer of Mortgage dated
is made between:
(1) the Lender
(2) the Borrower
(3) the Transferee

1 This deed is supplemental to a mortgage dated   and made between the Borrower and the Lender ('the Mortgage').

2 The Lender acknowledges the receipt from the Transferee of £   .

3 The Lender as beneficial owner assigns to the Transferee the benefit of the Mortgage.

4 The parties agree that all interest under the Mortgage has been paid to date and the outstanding principal is £   .[2]

1   See note 1 to precedent 86.

2   It is desirable that this clause is included as it establishes the state of the mortgage debt at the date of transfer. No warranty by the lender (as in precedent 86) is required as the Borrower is estopped from denying the amount of the outstanding capital.

88

Transfer of mortgage by the personal representative of of the mortgagee[1]

This Transfer of Mortgage dated
is made between:
(1) the Personal Representative
(2) the Transferee

1 This deed is supplemental to a mortgage dated *etc* ('the Mortgage').

2 On [*date*] the Principal [*or* the   District] Probate Registry granted to the Personal Representative [Probate of the Will] *or* [Letters of Administration of the estate] of [*deceased mortgagee*].

3 The Personal Representative acknowledges the receipt from the Transferee of £   .

4 The Personal Representative as personal representative assigns to the Transferee the benefit of the Mortgage.

5 The Personal Representative warrants that all interest under the Mortgage has been paid to date and the outstanding principal is £   .[2]

6 The Personal Representative acknowledges the right of the Transferee to the production of the grant of [Probate] *or* [Letters of Administration] referred to in clause 2 and to the supply of copies.

1   See note 1 to precedent 86.

The draftsman may prefer to specify the transferor as 'the Executor' or 'the Administrator' rather than as 'the Personal Representative'.

If the transferee is entitled to the mortgage under the will or intestacy of the deceased, it will be more usual for the personal representative to assent to its vesting in the transferee. See precedent 106.

If the borrower joins in the transfer, this precedent can be adapted by reference to precedent 87.

2   This will enable the transferee to sue the personal representative if the outstanding balance under the mortgage has been over-stated.

89

Vacating Receipt by the original mortgagee where the mortgage has been repaid by the original mortgagor[1]

I the within named   have received from the within named
all the money secured by this mortgage.
Date:
Signed: [*signature of mortgagee*]

1   This Vacating Receipt will operate under LPA 1925, s 115, the requirements of which are that:

   (a) The receipt is endorsed on, written at the foot of, or annexed to the mortgage;

   (b) The name of the payer is stated in the receipt, although this is not necessary in the case of a building society mortgage;

   (c) The payer is the person entitled to the immediate equity of redemption;

   (d) The receipt is executed by the person entitled to the mortgage (although the word 'executed' does not necessitate a deed).

If the above requirements are satisfied the receipt will extinguish the mortgage term or interest and will discharge the mortgaged property from all money secured by the mortgage. If the above requirements are not satisfied, the document will operate as a transfer of the mortgage unless a contrary intention is expressed.

When the mortgage consists of more than one deed, the receipt may be endorsed on, written at the foot of, or annexed to any one of the deeds, but it must refer either to all the deeds by which the mortgage money is secured or to the aggregate amount of the mortgage money actually owing. Where there is a further charge, therefore, various possibilities are available:—

   (a) The vacating receipt provided by this precedent with the addition of the words 'and a further charge dated *etc*' could be endorsed on the original mortgage;

   (b) A vacating receipt relating to the mortgage could be endorsed on the mortgage and one relating to the further charge on the further charge;

   (c) A vacating receipt could be endorsed on the further charge only, using the words 'secured by this deed and a mortgage dated *etc*'.

90

Vacating Receipt by the personal representative of the original mortgagee[1]

1 On   the [Principal] *or* [District] Probate Registry granted to me   of   [Probate of the Will] *or* [Letters of Administration of the estate] of the within named [*lender*].

2 I have received from the within named [*borrower*] all the money secured by this mortgage.[2]

3 I acknowledge the right of the within named [*borrower*] to the production of the Grant of [Probate] *or* [Letters of Administration] referred to above and to the supply of copies.

Date:

Signed: [*signature of personal representative*]

1   See note 1 to precedent 89.

2   Where part of the mortgage debt has been repaid during the lifetime of the deceased there can be substituted:
   I acknowledge that all the money secured by this mortgage has been received from the within named   .

91

Vacating Receipt by the personal representative of the survivor of the original mortgagees[1]

1 The within named   died on

2 The within named   died on

3 On   the [Principal] *or* [District] Probate Registry granted to me   of   [Probate of the Will] *or* [Letters of Administration] of the estate of the within named

          .

4 I have received from the within named   all the money secured by this mortgage.

5 I acknowledge the right of the within named   to the production of the Grant of [Probate] *or* [Letters of Administration] referred to above and to the supply of copies.
Date:
Signed: [*Signature of personal representative*]

1   See note 1 to Precedent 89 and note 2 to Precedent 90.

92

Vacating Receipt by survivor of joint mortgagees where the mortgage has been repaid by the original mortgagor[1]

I the within named   the survivor of myself and the within named   who died on   have received from the within named   all the money secured by this mortgage.

Date:

Signed: [*Signature of surviving mortgagee*]

1   See note 1 to Precedent 89.

93

Vacating receipt by original mortgagee where mortgage has been repaid by the survivor of joint mortgagors[1]

I the within named   have received from the within named
the survivor of himself and the within named   who died
on   all the money secured by this mortgage.
Date:
Signed: [*Signature of mortgagee*]

1   See note 1 to precedent 89.
It is immaterial whether the mortgagors were beneficial joint tenants or tenants in common because they must have been joint tenants of the legal estate and the surviving trustee is the person entitled to the immediate equity of redemption.

94

Vacating receipt by the transferee of the original mortgage[1]

I AB the transferee of this mortgage have received from the within
named ˙   all the money secured by this mortgage.
Date:
Signed: [*Signature of transferee*]

1   See note 1 to precedent 89. The vacating receipt must be endorsed on the mortgage and not the transfer.

It is not necessary to recite the details of the transfer as the borrower will have verified that the transferee has the benefit of the mortgage and the transfer itself will be handed over to the borrower.

95

Vacating Receipt by original mortgagee where mortgage has been repaid by the personal representative of the mortgagor[1]

I the within named   have received from AB the personal representative of the within named   all the money secured by this mortgage.

Date:

Signed: [*Signature of mortgagee*]

1   See note 1 to precedent 89.

It is not necessary to recite the grant of probate to the personal representative as this document constitutes an essential part of the title of the personal representative to the property after a redemption of the mortgage.

96

Vacating Receipt by original mortgagee where mortgage has been repaid by a person (other than the original mortgagor) entitled to the property charged[1]

I the within named   have received all the money secured by this mortgage from AB being the person entitled to the immediate equity of redemption in the property to which this mortgage relates.
Date:
Signed: [*Signature of mortgagee*]

1   See note 1 to precedent 89.

It is not necessary to recite details of the transfer of the mortgaged property as this deed will constitute an essential part of the title to the property of the transferee after the redemption of the mortgage.

97

Conveyance of property subject to a mortgage[1]

This Conveyance dated
is made between:
(1) the Vendor
(2) the Purchaser

By a deed dated *etc* ('the Mortgage') the Vendor mortgaged the land and house known as [*postal address*] ('the Property') which is fully described in a conveyance dated *etc*.

1 The Vendor acknowledges the receipt from the Purchaser of £   the purchase price of the Property.

2 The Vendor as beneficial owner conveys to the Purchaser the fee simple estate in the Property subject to the Mortgage.

3 The Purchaser covenants with the Vendor:

   (a) to pay all money secured by the Mortgage in accordance with the provisions of the Mortgage;

   (b) to observe the other provisions contained or implied in the Mortgage;

   (c) to indemnify the Vendor against all liabilities arising under the Mortgage.

4 The Vendor warrants that all interest due under the Mortgage has been paid and that the outstanding principal is £   .[2]

Add any appropriate standard clauses

Certificate of value (if applicable)

1 The vendor is entitled to convey the property without the consent of the lender unless there is an express prohibition in the mortgage. Where the lender is agreeable, however, it is desirable that he should join in the conveyance to release the vendor from the mortgage debt and precedent 98 is designed for this. If the lender is not a party to the deed, notice of the conveyance must be given to him.

If the property is subject to restrictive covenants, reference to these should be made in the conveyance and an indemnity clause included. See precedent 3.

2 This clause is desirable for two reasons. First, stamp duty is payable on the aggregate of the purchase price and the amount of the principal outstanding under the mortgage. Secondly, it enables the purchaser to sue the vendor on the warranty if the amount of principal has been understated.

98

Conveyance of property subject to a mortgage—the lender joining in to release the Vendor

This Conveyance dated
is made between:
(1) the Vendor
(2) the Lender
(3) the Purchaser

By a deed dated *etc* ('the Mortgage') the Vendor mortgaged to the Lender the land and house known as [*postal address*] ('the Property') which is full described in a conveyance dated *etc*.[1]

1 The Vendor acknowledges the receipt from the Purchaser of £   the purchase price of the Property.

2 The Vendor as beneficial owner conveys to the Purchaser the fee simple estate in the Property subject to the Mortgage.

3 The Purchaser covenants with the Lender to observe from the date of this deed all the provisions of the Mortgage as if he had been the original borrower.

4 The Lender releases the Vendor from all liabilities under the Mortgage except his implied covenants for title.[2]

5 The parties agree that all interest due under the Mortgage has been paid and that the outstanding principal is £   .[3]

Add any appropriate standard clauses

Certificate of value (if applicable)

1   If the property is subject to restrictive covenants, reference to these should be made in the conveyance and an indemnity clause included. See precedent 3.

2   The vendor should not be released from his implied covenants for title so that if, for example, the lender were to enforce his security and a defect in title became apparent, the lender could call on the vendor to execute a further assurance.

3   This clause is necessary because stamp duty is payable on the aggregate of the purchase price and the amount of the principal outstanding under the mortgage. It also establishes between the parties the state of the mortgage debt.

99

Conveyance of part of property subject to a mortgage—the lender joining in to release the part conveyed[1]

This Conveyance dated
is made between:
(1) the Vendor
(2) the Lender
(3) the Purchaser

By a deed dated *etc* ('the Mortgage') the Vendor mortgaged to the Lender (together with other property) the land and house known as [*postal address*] ('the Property') which is fully described in a conveyance dated *etc*.[1]

1 The Vendor acknowledges the receipt from the Purchaser of £   the purchaser price of the Property.[2]

2 The Vendor as beneficial owner conveys to the Purchaser the fee simple estate in the Property.

3 The Lender as mortgagee releases the Property from the Mortgage.

Add any appropriate standard clauses[3]

Certificate of value (if applicable)

1   If the property is subject to restrictive covenants, reference to this should be made in the conveyance and an indemnity clause included. See precedent 3.

2   If the whole or part of the purchase price is paid to the lender, traditional precedents state the facts in the deed. This is not necessary any more than it is necessary in a conveyance of the whole of the property subject to a mortgage to state that part of the purchase price is being paid to the lender to discharge the existing mortgage. The payment to the Lender can be adequately dealt with administratively by the parties' solicitors.

3   The acknowledgment for production will be in the form appropriate to property subject to a mortgage. See standard clauses, pp 292ff. An acknowledgment will be required for at least the mortgage deed.

100

Release of part of property subject to a mortgage

This Release dated
is made between:
(1) the Lender
(2) the Borrower

1 The property described in the first schedule is subject to a mortgage dated   and made between (1) the Borrower and (2) the Lender ('the Mortgage').

2 The Lender as mortgagee releases from the Mortgage the property described in the second schedule.

First Schedule

Description of the whole of the property subject to the Mortgage.

Second Schedule

Description of the property released.

101

Deed of Postponement regulating priorities between two mortgagees[1]

This Deed of Postponement dated
is made between:
(1) the Bank
(2) the Society

1   In this deed:

   (a) 'the Borrower' means   ;

   (b) 'the Property' means the land and house known as [*postal address*];

   (c) 'the existing Mortgage' means a legal charge [*or* mortgage] of the Property dated   and made between the Borrower and the Bank;

   (d) 'the new Mortgage' means a legal charge [*or* mortgage] relating to the Property to be concluded between the Borrower and the Society immediately after the execution of this deed and to bear the same date as this deed.

2   The Bank agrees with the Society that the Banks rights under the existing Mortgage in relation to the Property shall be postponed to the rights of the Society under the new Mortgage so that the new Mortgage shall rank in priority to the existing Mortgage.

1   For the sake of convenience it has been assumed, in this precedent, that the existing mortgage is in favour of a bank and the new mortgage to a building society.

The deed need only be sealed by the bank.

Presumably, as the original first mortgagees, the bank will hold the title deeds. By virtue of this deed, the bank will become second mortgagees and the title deeds ought, therefore, to be passed to the building society but probably the building society cannot insist on this.

It is desirable that a certified copy of the deed be placed with the existing Mortgage and, of course, it will be necessary for whichever of the lenders does not hold the title deeds to register its charge as a puisne mortgage under the Land Charges Act.

If the new Mortgage contains a provision for further advances then any such advances will also rank in priority to the existing Mortgage.

102

Deed postponing a second mortgage to a further charge in favour of the first mortgage[1]

This Deed of Postponement dated
is made between:
(1) the Bank
(2) the Society

1 In this deed:

(a) 'the Borrowers' means   ;

(b) 'the Property' means the land and house known as [*postal address*];

(c) 'the Second Mortgage' means a legal charge [*or* mortgage] of the Property dated   and made between the Borrowers and the Bank;

(d) 'the Further Charge' means a further charge relating to the Property to be concluded between the Borrowers and the Society immediately after the execution of this deed and to bear the same date as this deed.

2 The Bank agrees with the Society that the Banks rights under the Second Mortgage in relation to the Property shall be postponed to the rights of the Society under the Further Charge so that the Further Charge shall rank in priority to the Second Mortgage.

1   For the sake of convenience it has been assumed, in this precedent, that the second mortgage is in favour of a bank and the first mortgage and further charge in favour of a building society.

The deed need only be sealed by the bank. As the title deeds will already be in the possession of the society as first mortgagee and the second mortgage will already be registered as a puisne mortgage under the Land Charges Act, nothing further need be done except for a certified copy to be placed with the second mortgage.

103

Conveyance by mortgagee in exercise of his statutory power[1]

This Conveyance dated
is made between:
(1) the Vendor
(2) the Purchaser

By a deed dated *etc* ('the Mortgage') [*name of borrower*] mortgaged to the Vendor the land and house known as [*postal address*] ('the Property') which is fully described in a conveyance dated *etc*.

1 The Vendor acknowledges the receipt from the Purchaser of £   the purchase price of the Property.

2 The Vendor as mortgagee conveys to the Purchaser the fee simple estate in the Property.

Add any appropriate standard clauses

Certificate of value (if applicable)

1   The power of sale arises under LPA 1925, s 101(1)(i) once the mortgage money has become due but the power is exercisable only when the provisions of s 103 are satisfied. Section 101(3), however, permits both regulatory provisions to be varied or extended by the mortgage deed and s 104(2) and (3) protects the purchaser against an improper exercise of the power of sale *provided that the power of sale has arisen.*

Part 4 Assents

104

Assent by a personal representative vesting property in himself beneficially[1]

This Assent dated
is made by me
(A) At his death on [*name of deceased*] of   ('the Deceased')
was the owner of the property described in the schedule[2]
('the Property').
(B) On   the [Principal] *or* [District] Probate
Registry granted to me Probate of the Will[3] of the Deceased ('the
Grant').

1   I assent to the estate in the Property held by the Deceased[4] vesting in
me.

2   I acknowledge the right of my successors in title to the production of
the Grant and to the supply of copies.[5]

Schedule

Description of Property

1   AEA 1925, s 36 confers on personal representatives the power to assent to property vesting 'in any person who (whether by devise, bequest, devolution, appropriation or otherwise) may be entitled thereto, either beneficially or as trustee or as a personal representative'. These powers are wide enough to include an assent in favour of a purchaser from a beneficiary but, in those circumstances, it is better to assent to the beneficiary, leaving him to convey the property to the purchaser.

If the Assent is to pass a legal estate it must be in writing, signed by the personal representative and name the person in whose favour it is made. It need not be under seal unless the assentee gives covenants. In either case no stamp duty is payable.

The assentee can require notice of the Assent to be endorsed on the grant of representation. The section provides that a statement in writing by a personal representative that he has not given or made an assent or conveyance in respect of a legal estate is, in favour of a purchaser, sufficient evidence that there has been no assent or conveyance *unless notice of it appears on or is annexed to the grant*. The memorandum, therefore, need only give the information necessary to warn off a prospective purchaser and so can be quite short, for example:

By an Assent dated   the property known as [*postal address or short description if no postal address*] was vested in [*name*].

2   If the property can conveniently be described by reference to the postal address such as:

the land and house known as   [which is fully described in a conveyance dated *etc*] ('the Property')

the use of a schedule can be avoided.

3   Or 'Letters of Administration of the estate' as the case may be.

4   Usually it is not the duty of a personal representative's solicitor to investigate the deceased's title to the property. He may not be willing therefore to draw the assent in terms that express the estate of the deceased to be a fee simple or a leasehold in case it transpires that the title of the deceased was defective. This consideration does not apply to the same extent where the assent is in favour of the personal representative himself. See next precedent for an alternative form.

5   Although, logically, a personal representative cannot acknowledge his own right to production, he can acknowledge the right of his successors.

105

Assent by a personal representative vesting property in himself beneficially—alternative form[1]

This Assent dated
is made by me
(A) At his death [*name of deceased*] of   ('the Deceased') was the owner of the property described in the schedule[2] ('the Property').
(B) On   the [Principal] *or* [District] Probate Registry granted to me Probate of the Will[3] of the Deceased ('the Grant').

1 I assent to the fee simple estate in the Property vesting in me.[4]

2 I acknowledge the right of my successors in title to the production of the Grant and to the supply of copies.[5]

Schedule

Description of Property

1 See note 1 to precedent 104.

2 If the property can conveniently be described by reference to the postal address such as:

    the land and house known as   [which is fully described in a conveyance
    dated *etc*] ('the Property')
the use of a schedule can be avoided.

3 Or 'Letters of Administration of the estate' as the case may be.

4 Usually it is not the duty of a personal representative's solicitor to investigate the deceased's title to the property. He may not be willing therefore to draw the assent in terms that express the estate of the deceased to be a fee simple or a leasehold in case it transpires that the title of the deceased was defective. See preceding precedent. This consideration does not apply to the same extent where the assent is in favour of the personal representative himself.

5 Although, logically, a person representative cannot acknowledge his own right to production, he can acknowledge the right of his successors.

106

Assent by a personal representative in favour of a beneficiary[1]

This Assent dated
is made between:
(1) the Executor[2]
(2) the Beneficiary
(A) At his death on [*name of deceased*] of   ('the Deceased')
was the owner of the property described in the schedule[3] ('the Property').
(B) On   the [Principal] *or* [District] Probate
Registry granted to the Executor Probate of the Will[4] of the Deceased
('the Grant').

1 The Executor as personal representative[5] assents to the estate in the Property held by the Deceased[6] vesting in the Beneficiary.

2 The Executor acknowledges the right of the Beneficiary to the production of the Grant and to the supply of copies.

Schedule

Description of Property

1   See note 1 to precedent 104.

2   Or 'the Administrator' as the case may be.

3   If the property can conveniently be described by reference to the postal address such as:
    the land and house known as   [which is fully described in a conveyance
    dated *etc*] ('the Property')
the use of a schedule can be avoided.

4   Or 'Letters of Administration of the estate' as the case may be.

5   The words 'as personal representative' will imply the same covenant as when they are in a conveyance. See AEA 1925, s 36(3); LPA 1925, s 76(1)(F) and Schedule 2 Part VI.

6   Usually it is not the duty of a personal representative's solicitor to investigate the deceased's title to the property. He may not be willing therefore to draw the assent in terms that express the estate of the deceased to be a fee simple or a leasehold in case it transpires that the title of the deceased was defective. If the draftsman has no such reservations, this clause can be amended to read:
    The Executor as personal representative assents to the fee simple estate in the
    Property vesting in the Beneficiary.

107

Assent by executors to themselves as trustees for sale[1]

This Assent dated
is made by us
(A) At his death on [*name of deceased*] of   ('the Deceased')
was the owner of the property described in the schedule[2] ('the Property').
(B) On   the [Principal] *or* [District] Probate
Registry granted to us Probate of the Will of the Deceased ('the Grant').

1   As personal representatives[3] we assent to the fee simple estate in the
Property vesting in ourselves as trustees on the trust for sale concerning
the Property contained in the Will of the Deceased dated   .[4]

2   We acknowledge the right of our successors in title to the production
of the Grant and to the supply of copies.[5]

Schedule

Description of Property

1　See note 1 to precedent 104.

2　If the property can conveniently be described by reference to the postal address such as:

　　the land and house known as　　　　　　[which is fully described in a conveyance
　　dated *etc*] ('the Property')

the use of a schedule can be avoided.

3　The words 'as personal representatives' will imply the same covenant as when they are used in a conveyance. See AEA 1925, s 36(3), LPA 1925, s 76(1)(F) and Schedule 2 Part IV.

4　Probably the reference to the Will could be omitted but it is thought to be a better practice to specify the trust instrument rather than merely to state 'we assent to the fee simple estate in the Property vesting in ourselves as trustees for sale'.

5　Although, logically, a personal representative cannot acknowledge his right to production, he can acknowledge the right of his successors.

108

Assent by executors vesting property in others as trustees for sale[1]

This Assent dated
is made between:
(1) the Executors
(2) the Trustees
(A) At his death on [*name of deceased*] of   ('the Deceased')
was the owner of the property described in the schedule[2] ('the Property').
(B) On   the [Principal] *or* [District] Probate
Registry granted to the Executors Probate of the Will of the Deceased
('the Grant').

1   The Executors as personal representatives[3] assent to the estate in the
Property held by the Deceased[4] vesting in the Trustees on the trust for
sale concerning the Property contained in the Will of the Deceased dated

2   The Executors acknowledge the right of the Trustees to the production
of the Grant and to the supply of copies.

Schedule

Description of Property

1   See note 1 to precedent 104.

2   If the Property can conveniently be described by reference to the postal address such as:

the land and house known as   [which is fully described in a conveyance
dated *etc*] ('the Property')
the use of a schedule can be avoided.

3   The words 'as personal representatives' will imply the same covenant as when they are used in a conveyance. See AEA 1925, s 36(3), LPA 1925, s 76(1)(F) and Schedule 2 Part VI.

4   Usually it is not the duty of a personal representative's solicitor to investigate the deceased's title to the property. He may not be willing therefore to draw the assent in terms that express the estate of the deceased to be a fee simple or a leasehold in case it transpires that the title of the deceased was defective. If the draftsman has no such reservations, this clause can be amended to refer to the fee simple estate in the Property vesting in the Trustees.

109

Assent by a personal representative in favour of a beneficiary of property subject to an existing mortgage[1]

This Assent dated
is made between:
(1) the Executor[2]
(2) the Beneficiary
(A) At his death on [*name of deceased*] of   ('the Deceased')
was the owner of the property described in the schedule[3] ('the Property')
subject to a mortgage dated   and made between the Deceased
and   ('the Mortgage').
(B) On   the [Principal] *or* [District] Probate
Registry granted to the Executor Probate of the Will[4] of the Deceased
('the Grant').

1   The Executor as personal representative[5] assents to the estate in the
Property held by the Deceased[6] vesting in the Beneficiary subject to the
Mortgage.

or

1   The executor as personal representative assents to the fee simple
estate in the Property vesting in the Beneficiary subject to the Mortgage.

2   The Beneficiary covenants with the Executor:[7]

(a) to pay all money secured by the Mortgage in accordance with the
provisions of the Mortgage;

(b) to observe the other provisions contained or implied in the
Mortgage;

(c) to indemnify the Executor against all liabilities under the
Mortgage.

3   The Executor acknowledges the right of the Beneficiary to the
production of the Grant and to the supply of copies.

Schedule

Description of Property

1   See note 1 to precedent 104.

2   Or 'the Administrator' as the case may be.

3   If the property can conveniently be described by reference to the postal address such as:

the land and house known as   [which is fully described in a conveyance
dated *etc*] ('the Property')

the use of a schedule can be avoided.

4   Or 'Letters of Administration of the estate' as the case may be.

5   The words 'as personal representative' will imply the same covenant as when they are used in a conveyance. See AEA 1925, s 36(3), LPA 1925, s 76(1)(F) and Schedule 2 Part VI.

6   Usually it is not the duty of a personal representative's solicitor to investigate the deceased's title to the property. He may not be willing therefore to draw the assent in terms that express the estate of the deceased to be a fee simple or a leasehold in case it transpires that the title of the deceased was defective. If the draftsman has no such reservations, the clause can be amended to refer to the fee simple estate vesting in the Beneficiary.

7   The inclusion of this clause requires the Assent to be under seal and executed by both parties. Strictly, there is no need for the beneficiary to covenant in the terms set out because he must take the property subject to any incumbrances affecting it. It is good practice, however, to include an express covenant because it draws the attention of the beneficiary to his obligations and simplifies the task of the personal representative in the event of his being sued by the lender. He can then join the beneficiary in the action and seek indemnity under the covenant. In the absence of an express covenant, the personal representative would have to plead an equitable indemnity. Where there are onerous provisions affecting the property, it is desirable that the beneficiary should sign the document, even where no express covenant is included, since it will prevent his alleging subsequently that he had disclaimed.

110

Assent by a personal representative relating to leasehold property or property subject to a rentcharge[1]

This Assent dated
is made between:
(1) the Executor[2]
(2) the Beneficiary
(A) At his death on [*name of deceased*] of   ('the Deceased')
was the owner of the property described in the schedule ('the Property').
(B) On   the [Principal] *or* [District] Probate
Registry granted to the Executor Probate of the Will[3] of the Deceased.

1 The Executor as personal representative assents to the leasehold estate in the Property vesting in the Beneficiary.

2 The Beneficiary covenants with the Executor:[4]

(a) to pay the yearly rent and perform and observe the covenants and restrictions to which the Property is subject;

(b) to indemnify the Executor against any liability resulting from a breach of this covenant.

3 The Executor acknowledges the right of the Beneficiary to the production of the Grant and to the supply of copies.

Schedule[5]

The land and house known as [*postal address*] which is fully described in a lease dated *etc* subject to a yearly ground rent of £   made payable by the lease and to such covenants and restrictions contained in it as are still effective

or

The land and house known as [*postal address*] which is fully described in an assignment dated *etc* ('the Assignment') subject to:

(a) an apportioned yearly ground rent of £   made payable by the Assignment;

(b) such covenants and restrictions contained in a lease dated *etc* as are still effective and relate to the Property;

(c) the agreements declarations covenants and charges by [*the assignee named in the Assignment*] contained or implied in the Assignment.

or

The land and house known as [*postal address*] being the whole of the

1   See note 1 to precedent 104.
This precedent can easily be adapted to freehold property subject to a rentcharge.

2   Or 'the Administrator' as the case may be.

3   Or 'Letters of Administration of the estate' as the case may be.

4   The inclusion of this clause requires the assent to be under seal and executed by both parties. Strictly, there is no need for the beneficiary to covenant in the terms set out because he must take the property subject to any incumbrances affecting it. It is good practice, however, to include an express covenant because it draws the attention of the beneficiary to his obligations and simplifies the task of the personal representative in the event of his being sued by the freehold reversioner. He can then join the beneficiary in the action and seek indemnity under the covenant. In the absence of an express covenant, the personal representative would have to plead an equitable indemnity. Where there are onerous provisions affecting the property it is desirable that the beneficiary should sign the document, even where no express covenant is included, since it will prevent his alleging subsequently that he had disclaimed.
Subject to the observations in the preceding paragraph relating to good practice, it would be perfectly adequate for precedent 106 to be used for leasehold property or for property subject to a rentcharge.
5   The three descriptions are intended to cover cases in which the Assent relates to:
    (a) the whole of the property comprised in the lease;
    (b) a part that has been sold off; or
    (c) the residue after a previous sale-off.

property demised by a lease dated *etc* except such part as was comprised in an assignment dated *etc* ('the Assignment') subject to:

(a) an apportioned yearly ground rent of £   made payable by the Assignment;

(b) such covenants and restrictions contained in a lease dated *etc* as are still effective and relate to the Property;

(c) the agreements declarations covenants and charges by [*the assignor named in the Assignment*] contained or implied in the Assignment.

Part 5   Miscellaneous

111

Assignment of a life interest or other equitable interest[1]

This Assignment dated
is made between:
(1) the Vendor
(2) the Purchaser
The Vendor is beneficially entitled to a life interest in the land and house
known as [*postal address*] ('the Property') which is fully described in a
conveyance dated *etc*.

1 The Vendor acknowledges the receipt from the Purchaser of £
the purchase price of the interest assigned by this deed.

2 The Vendor as beneficial owner assigns to the Purchaser his life
interest in the Property.

Add any appropriate standard clauses

Certificate for value (if applicable)

1   A life interest (or any other equitable interest) can only subsist under a strict settlement or a trust for sale. Notice of the assignment should, therefore, be given to the trustees.

The precedent can easily be adapted for a life interest under a settlement or a Will or for an equitable interest other than a life interest, for example, a tenancy in common, by changing the recital, with consequential changes to the operative part of the deed, as follows:

> The Vendor is beneficially entitled to a life interest in the capital of a settlement
> dated *etc*   ('the Settlement)

or

> The Vendor is entitled to a life interest in the residuary estate of AB deceased

or

> The Vendor is beneficially entitled to a [one half] share in the land and house known
> as [*postal address*] ('the Property') which is fully described in a conveyance *etc*

112

Assignment of a remainder expectant on a life interest[1]

This Assignment dated
is made between:
(1) the Vendor
(2) the Purchaser
The Vendor is beneficially entitled to the land and house known as
[*postal address*] ('the Property') which is fully described in a conveyance
dated *etc* and which is subject to an existing life interest in favour of
another.

1 The Vendor acknowledges the receipt of £   the purchase
price of the interest transferred by this deed.

2 The Vendor as beneficial owner assigns to the Purchaser his beneficial
interest in the Property.

Add any appropriate standard clauses

Certificate of value (if applicable)

1   Notice of the assignment should be given to the trustees of the strict settlement or trust for sale under which the life interest subsists. Upon the death of the life tenant it will be necessary for the legal estate in the property to be vested in the assignee either by the trustees of the settlement or the personal representatives of the tenant for life. This can be done either by an assent or a conveyance.

This precedent can be adapted for the assignment of an interest in remainder of a trust fund by using a recital along the lines set out below with consequential changes to the operative part of the deed.

The Vendor is beneficially entitled to [a one third share] in the residuary estate of AB deceased which is subject to an existing life interest in favour of another

or

The Vendor is beneficially entitled to [share in] the capital fund of a settlement dated *etc* ('the Settlement') which is subject to an existing life interest in favour of another

113

Clause limiting Vendor's liability under implied covenants relating to the state and condition of the property[1]

Any covenants by the Vendor implied by statute in this deed [as a result of the Vendor assigning as beneficial owner][2] shall not extend to the breach of any covenant contained in the Lease [*or* Underlease] relating to the state and condition of the Property.[3]

1   This clause is intended to accommodate the requirements of standard conditions of sale.

The Law Society's General Conditions of Sale (1984 revision) provide in relation to leaseholds:

> 8(5) Any statutory implied covenants on the part of the vendor shall not extend to any breach of the terms of the lease as to the state and condition of the property and the assignment shall so provide. This sub-condition applies notwithstanding that a special condition provides for the vendor to convey as beneficial owner.

The National Conditions of Sale (20th edition) provide in relation to leaseholds:

> 11(7) Any statutory covenant to be implied in the conveyance on the part of the vendor shall be so limited as not to affect him with liability for a subsisting breach of any covenant or condition concerning the state or condition of the property of which state and condition the purchaser is by paragraph (3) of condition 13 deemed to have full notice.

and condition 13(3) provides:

> The purchaser shall be deemed to buy with full notice in all respects of the actual state and condition of the property and, save where it is to be constructed or converted by the vendor, shall take the property as it is.

Presumably the purchaser could insist on the limitation relating to the state and condition of the property *at the date of the contract* but, in practice, he is unlikely to do so.

2   To be inserted if the Vendor has assigned as beneficial owner.

Care should be taken where beneficial owner covenants are expressly incorporated for example by a clause such as:

> The same covenants shall be incorporated in this deed as would have been implied if the Vendors being beneficial owners had been expressed to convey as beneficial owners

In these circumstances this precedent will not be suitable because the covenants are not implied by statute but incorporated by the parties and the following words should then be added to the above clause:

> but those covenants shall not extend to the breach of any covenant contained in the Lease [*or* Underlease] relating to the state and condition of the Property.

3   If so defined.

114

Clause relating to easements in favour of property retained by the Vendor after a sale-off[1, 2]

Except and Reserved from this conveyance such rights over the Property[2] as would have been implied in favour of the Retained Premises[2] if simultaneously with this conveyance the Vendor had conveyed the Retained Premises[3] to somebody other than the Purchaser.

1   This clause is intended to accommodate the requirements of standard conditions of sale.

The Law Society's General Conditions of Sale (1984 revision) provide:

5(3)(a) In this sub-condition 'the retained land' means land retained by the Vendor—
  (i) adjoining the property, or
  (ii) near to the property and designated as retained land in a special condition.

(b) The conveyance of the property shall contain such reservations in favour of the retained land and the grant of such rights over the retained land as would have been implied had the Vendor conveyed both the property and the retained land by simultaneous conveyances to different purchasers.

The National Conditions of Sale (20th edition) provide:

20 Where the property and any adjacent or neighbouring property have hitherto been in common ownership, the purchaser shall not become entitled to any right to light or air over or in respect of any adjacent or neighbouring property which is retained by the Vendor and the Conveyance shall, if the Vendor so requires, reserve to him such easements and rights as would become appurtenant to such last-mentioned property by implication of law if the Vendor had sold it to another purchaser at the same time as he had sold the property to the purchaser.

2   See also Appendix (pp 299ff).

3   If so defined. The grant of corresponding easements will be implied. See Appendix (pp 299ff).

Standard Clauses

A Acknowledgment by beneficial owner[1]
The Vendor undertakes with the Purchaser to keep safe the documents listed in the schedule and acknowledges the right of the Purchaser to their production and to the supply of copies.

B Acknowledgment by Trustees etc[2]
The Vendors acknowledge the right of the Purchaser to the production of the documents listed in the schedule and to the supply of copies.

C Acknowledgment by personal representative[3]
The Vendor acknowledges the right of the Purchaser to the production of the grant of [Probate] referred to above and to the supply of copies.

D Acknowledgment by Mortgagee[4]
(a) The Lender acknowledges the right of the Purchaser to the production of the documents listed in the schedule and to the supplies of copies;
(b) The Vendor covenants with the Purchaser that when these documents come into his possession he will if required and on payment of his costs execute a statutory undertaking for their safe custody.

E Indemnity against breach of covenants[5]
The Purchaser covenants with the Vendor to indemnify the Vendor against liability resulting from future breach or non-observance of the covenants and restrictions [referred to in clause   ] of this deed *or* [contained or referred to in a conveyance dated *etc*] *or* [to which the Property is subject]

or

The Purchaser covenants with the Vendor by way of indemnity only to perform and observe the covenants and restrictions [referred to in clause   of this deed] *or* [contained or referred to in a conveyance dated *etc*] *or* [to which the Property is subject] and to indemnify the Vendor against liability resulting from any future breach or non-observance.

F Certificate of value[6]
It is certified that this transaction does not form part of a larger transaction or of a series of transactions in respect of which the amount or value or the aggregate amount or value of the consideration exceeds £   .

G Certificate for value—exempt instrument[7]
It is certified that this instrument falls within category   in the schedule to the Stamp Duty (Exempt Instruments) Regulations 1987.

1   See LPA 1925, s 64. In the traditional form, the undertaking for safe custody follows the acknowledgment for production. Here the order has been reversed, chiefly for the sake of euphony, although it can be said to be a more logical order as the vendor must keep the documents safe in order to be able to produce them.

2   It is not customary for a trustee to give an undertaking for safe custody.

3   It is not customary for a personal representative to give an undertaking for safe custody. If the undertaking extends to documents other than the grant of representation, it is preferable to schedule the documents.

4   It is not customary for mortgagees to give an undertaking for safe custody. Clause (b) is the traditional method of the purchaser's obtaining an undertaking for safe custody. In practice the purchaser never calls for the undertaking for safe custody to be executed unless the documents have been lost by the vendor after coming into his possession. Although it would not constitute an 'undertaking for safe custody' within the provisions of s 64 it is tempting to substitute for clauses (b):

the Vendor undertakes that he will keep safe these documents when they come into his possession.

5   In most cases, the first clause will provide a sufficient indemnity. It does, however, confer only a right to be indemnified against damages recovered by the person entitled to the benefit of the covenants. The alternative clause goes further and enables the vendor to apply for an injunction to restrain a breach or threatened breach for which he could be liable to the person entitled to the benefit of the covenant.

6   The amount to be inserted will be governed by the current Finance Act.

7   Instruments specified in the Schedule to the Stamp Duty (Exempt Instruments) Regulations 1987 are exempt from stamp duty and no longer need to be produced to the Stamp Office for adjudication or any other purpose provided that this clause is included. The exempt categories are designated by capital letters and can be summarised as follows:

A   vesting of property on the appointment of new trustee;

B   conveyance to a specific devisee or legatee or his nominee;

C   conveyance to person entitled under intestacy or his nominee;

D   appropriation in satisfaction of a general pecuniary legacy or the interest of a surviving spouse;

E   conveyance to residuary beneficiary or his nominee;

F   conveyance constituting a distribution of property under the terms of a settlement;

G   conveyance in consideration of marriage to or for the benefit of a party to the marriage;

H   conveyance arising in connection with divorce or the settlement of a dispute relating to matrimonial proceedings;

I   conveyance by a liquidator to a shareholder or his nominee in satisfaction of his rights on the winding up;

J   grant of an easement for nil consideration;

K   [applies only to Scotland];

L   gift inter vivos;

M   conveyance under deed of family arrangement varying the dispositions under a will or intestacy.

H   Executions and Attestations
Normal attestation
Signed sealed and delivered by [the Vendor] in the presence of:

I   Execution by a Limited Company
The common seal of [the Vendor] was affixed to this deed in the presence of:

Director
Secretary

J   Execution under a Power of Attorney[8]
Signed sealed and delivered by AB on behalf of [the Vendor] by virtue of a Power of Attorney dated   in the presence of:

K   Execution by a Person Unable to Read or Write
After I had read and explained the contents of the above deed to [the Vendor] and he informed me that he understood it he signed sealed and delivered this deed by making his mark in my presence

L   Execution by a Person Unable to Write[9]
[the Vendor' being unable to write signed sealed and delivered this deed by making his mark in my presence

M   Execution by a Blind Person
After I had read the above deed to [the Vendor] (who is blind) and he had informed me that he understood it, he signed sealed and delivered this deed in my presence

N   Joint ownership clauses[10]
The Purchasers declare that they are beneficial joint tenants
or
The Purchasers declare that they are tenants in common in equal shares
or
The Purchasers declare that they are tenants in common in the following shares: AB three-fifths and CD two-fifths
or
The Purchasers declare that they are tenants in common in the proportions in which the purchase money was provided namely £
by AB and £   by CD
or
The Purchasers declare that they hold the Property on the trusts set out in a deed dated *etc*
or
The Purchasers declare that they hold the Property on the trusts of the Will of AB dated

8   The alternative of the ordinary form of attestation 'signed sealed and delivered by [the Vendor] in the presence of' can be used and the attorney can execute the deed 'AB by his attorney XY'.

The Powers of Attorney Act 1961 has greatly simplified the law relating to powers of attorney and extended the protection available to the grantees of conveyances executed under a power of attorney. The purchaser will require to be supplied with a photostat copy of the power of attorney certified in accordance with the Act and so there is no need to refer to the date etc of the power of attorney in the conveyance itself.

9   Where the incapacity is of a temporary nature, for example, as a result of a fractured wrist, it is desirable that this fact be stated by using words such as 'being temporarily unable to write because of injury'. The circumstances may be that the person executing the deed is able to write but his signature will be unlike his usual signature. In that case, the following clause is suggested:

This deed was signed sealed and delivered by [the Vendor] in my presence but because of [an injury to his right arm] his signature differs from his usual signature

10   Where the purchasers are also beneficially entitled to the property they will, of course, be joint tenants in law. In the first edition of this book, their beneficial ownership was described as being 'in equity'. The present editors have avoided this expression. Because the purchasers are legal joint tenants, it has been thought appropriate to describe them as *beneficial* joint tenants in the declaration relating to their beneficial joint tenancy. The declaration relating to an equitable tenancy in common does not require the use of the word 'beneficial' because it can only relate to the purchasers' beneficial interest.

O   Declaration relating to party walls and common easements[11]
The parties declare that:
(a) any wall fence or hedge separating the [*property conveyed*] from the adjoining land and house known as [*postal address*] ('the Retained Premises') shall be a party structure to be repaired and maintained at the equally shared expense of its owners;
(b) any sewers drains electricity cables gas pipes gutters downspouts and similar conduits serving both the [*property conveyed*] and the Retained Premises shall continue to be used as they were prior to the date of this deed [and shall be repaired and maintained at the equally shared expense of the owners of the [*property conveyed*] and the Retained Premises].

11   Most draftsmen make provision for the cost of repairing and maintaining party structures to be borne by the parties in equal shares, as in paragraph (a). The cost of rebuilding, say a party wall could be expensive. Moreover, neither party is likely to undertake the work without the other contributing to its cost. The same considerations do not apply to conduits. Some draftsmen prefer to make no provision for their maintenance, relying on the fact that the owner of each house is likely to undertake the repair of conduits on or under his own property and that, in many cases, it is hardly worth seeking a contribution. Different considerations would apply however to, say, a private sewer serving the two houses. In some circumstances, it may be proper to provide for the contribution to repairs to be in unequal shares. Whenever possible, however, it is preferable to define the contribution of the parties rather than make provision for the payment of a 'fair proportion of the cost' which can be a fruitful source of dispute in the future.

Appendix

Conveyance or assignment of part of property owned by the Vendor

Consideration must always be given to what rights are to be granted to the purchaser and what rights reserved to the vendor. It is better conveyancing practice to make express provision for the precise rights to be granted and excepted than to resort to rather vague generalities. In the case of houses or building land, obvious considerations are the use of sewers, drains, gutters, downspouts and other conduits, the right to tie into existing sewers etc and the right of the vendor to tie into and use sewers etc to be laid beneath the land conveyed (bearing in mind that such a right must be limited to the perpetuity period). What can in fact be granted to a purchaser will sometimes be governed by what has been excepted from conveyances effecting previous sales-off. Consequently, practical considerations may overrule desirability.

In addition to any rights expressly granted, the purchaser will obtain, unless a contrary intention is expressed in the deed, the following rights:

(1) Easements of necessity. See *Barry v Hasseldine* [1952] Ch 835, [1952] 2 All ER 317;
(2) Continuous and apparent easements that are necessary to the reasonable enjoyment of the property conveyed. See *Wheeldon v Burrows* (1878) 12 Ch D 31;
(3) Rights passing under LPA 1925, s 62.

On the other hand, the vendor will retain only easements of necessity and rights expressly reserved. These considerations should be at the forefront of the draftsman's mind when deciding what rights should be expressly granted and reserved. The provisions of LPA 1925, s 62 are very wide and are thought by some to be too wide. Where it is the intention of the vendor that certain rights governed by this section should not pass to the purchaser, care should be taken that an appropriate provision is made in the contract, otherwise the vendor will not be entitled to insist on the operation of s 62 being limited by the assignment.

Rights will pass to the purchaser by implied grant under *Wheeldon v Burrows* but similar rights will not be reserved to the vendor by implication, for example, a right of light. See *Liddiard v Waldron* [1934] 1 KB 425, [1933] All ER 276 and *Ray v Hazeldine* [1904] 2 Ch 17. For exceptions to the rule that there will be no implied reservations of an easement or quasi-easement in favour of the vendor, see *Aldridge v Wright* [1929] 2 KB 117 per Greer LJ.

While the draftsman has been counselled against using a form of words of general application, sometimes it is necessary and the following, adapted if necessary, may be useful in some cases:

There is excepted and reserved from this conveyance any easement quasi-easement or right that prior to the date of his deed was enjoyed by the Vendor for the benefit of the [retained premises] and which continues to be necessary to the reasonable enjoyment of the [retained premises].

The purchaser's position is adequately covered without any corresponding clause in his favour.

Where, at the same time, part of the land is sold to one purchaser and the remainder to another, *Wheeldon v Burrows* applies to both transactions and both the Law Society's Conditions of Sale (1984 Revision) and the National Conditions of Sale (20th edition 1981) take advantage of this.

Clause 5(3) of the Law Society's Conditions of Sale provides:

(a) In this sub-condition "the retained land" means land retained by the vendor
   (i) adjoining the property, or
   (ii) near to the property and designated as retained land in a special condition
(b) The conveyance of the property shall contain such reservations in favour of the retained land and the grant of such rights over the retained land as would have been implied had the vendor conveyed both the property and the retained land by simultaneous conveyances to different purchasers.

Clause 20 of the National Conditions of Sale provides:

Where the property and any adjacent or neighbouring property have hitherto been in common ownership, the purchaser shall not become entitled to any right to light or air over or in respect of any adjacent or neighbouring property which is retained by the vendor and the conveyance shall, if the vendor so requires, reserve to him such easements and rights as would become appurtenant to such last-mentioned property by implication of law, if the vendor had sold it to another purchaser at the same time as he has sold the property to the purchaser.

Although a substantial majority of contracts for sale are governed by one or other of these Conditions, purchasers' solicitors often draft the assurance without regard to the above provision and, not infrequently, the vendor's solicitor is content with a clause limited to party walls and to gutters and downspouts serving both properties. This is unwise unless there are no other quasi-easements that the vendor has assumed will continue to benefit the retained premises. To give effect to the simultaneous sale device used by the Conditions of Sale, one of the clauses set out below can be used instead of the suggested clause excepting easements quasi-easements and other rights in favour of the retained premises.

In the case of the Law Society's Conditions:

There shall be incorporated in this deed
(a) the grant of rights in favour of [the Property] and
(b) the reservation of rights in favour of [the retained premises]
such as would have been implied if the Vendor had conveyed [the Property] to the Purchaser and at the same time conveyed [the retained premises] to another person.

and in the case of the National Conditions:

(a) The Purchaser shall not become entitled to any right of light or air over [the retained premises].
(b) There is reserved to the Vendor those easements and rights that would have become appurtenant to [the retained premises] if the Vendor had conveyed [the retained premises] to another purchaser at the same time as conveying [the Property] to the Purchaser.

As the grant of quasi-easements is implied by *Wheeldon v Burrows*, an express grant of such rights is not really necessary. Precedent 114 provides an alternative shorter version of the above clauses. A duplicate conveyance should be executed and a memorandum of the sale-off endorsed on the conveyance to the vendor. This memorandum is only a precautionary measure and the purchaser cannot insist on it unless provision is made in the contract. The following short form is sufficient:

By a conveyance dated [*date*] the house [*postal address*] was conveyed [*or* assigned] by [*the vendor*] to [*the purchaser*]

Conveyance of part of property affected by a rentcharge

Where the conveyance is for valuable consideration, covenants by the purchaser for the payment of the apportioned rent, for the performance of the grantees' covenants and for indemnity will be implied by LPA, s 77(1)(B). Where the conveyance is not for valuation consideration and these covenants are required the following clause may be used:

The same covenants and provisions shall be implied in this deed as if this conveyance had been for valuation consideration.

In addition to the personal covenants, LPA 1925, s 190(1) gives the parties mutual rights of distress if the conveyance is for valuable consideration. These rights attach to the land and bind the land in the hands of successors in title. Where the conveyance is not for valuable consideration, the use of the above clause, which includes the words 'and provisions' will incorporate s 190(1) as well as s 77(1)(B).

Where the vendor conveys or is expressed to convey as beneficial owner and the conveyance is for valuable consideration, covenants by the vendor to pay the residue of the rent, to perform the grantees covenants and for indemnity will be implied by LPA 1925, s 77(1)(B). If the vendor is not in fact a beneficial owner, sub-s (4) permits the section to be brought into operation by express reference to it. The following clause may be used:

The covenants referred to in section 77 of the Law of Property Act 1925 shall be implied in this deed as if the Vendor has been expressed to convey as beneficial owner.

The covenants would be implied by the vendor conveying as beneficial owner but that could also result in the covenants under LPA 1925, s 76 being implied. A vendor who is not a beneficial owner may be willing to give s 77 covenants relating to land retained by him but not the s 76 covenants relating to title.

LPA 1925, s 76 provides that where the vendor 'conveys *and* is expressed to convey as beneficial owner' covenants for title will be implied. Section 77 provides that covenants relating to rent and existing covenants will be implied where the vendor 'conveys *or* is expressed to convey as beneficial owner'. Some commentators contend that s 76 covenants will not be implied unless the vendor is in fact a beneficial owner of the legal estate and is also expressed to convey as beneficial owner. Others consider that s 76 covenants will be implied by the vendor being expressed to convey as beneficial owner whether or not he is a beneficial owner.

This uncertainty still exists although the LPA has been in force for over 60 years. It is suggested, therefore, that if a vendor who is not a beneficial owner is willing to give both s 76 and s 77 covenants the following clause should be used rather than the vendor being expressed to convey as beneficial owner:

The covenants that would have been implied in this deed if the Vendor had been a beneficial owner and had been expressed to convey as beneficial owner are expressly incorporated.

A duplicate conveyance should be executed and a memorandum of the sale-off endorsed on both the rentcharge deed (if in the vendor's possession) and the conveyance to the vendor (if he is not the original grantee). See suggested memorandum at the end of the preceding section.

Assignment of part of property affected by a ground rent

Where the assignment is for valuable consideration there will be covenants for payment of the apportioned ground rent, for the performance of the lessees covenants and for indemnity implied by LPA, s 77(1)(D). In addition, LPA 1925, s 190(3) will give mutual rights of distress. In other cases these covenants and provisions can be incorporated by the use of the following clause:

> The same covenants and provisions shall be implied in this deed as if this assignment had been for valuable consideration

Where the vendor assigns or is expressed to assign as beneficial owner (and the assignment is for valuable consideration) covenants by the vendor to pay the residue of the ground rent, to perform the lessees covenants and for indemnity will be implied by LPA 1925, s 77(1)(D). If the vendor is not a beneficial owner the covenants can be incorporated by using the following clause:

> The covenants referred to in section 77 of the Law of Property Act 1925 shall be implied in this deed as if the vendor had been expressed to assign as beneficial owner

Please refer to the preceding section where the effect of the vendor's assigning as beneficial owner in relation to s 76 covenants is discussed.

A duplicate assignment should be executed and a memorandum of the sale-off endorsed on the lease (if in the vendor's possession) and the assignment to the vendor (if he was not the original lessee). Please refer to the end of the first section for the form of memorandum.

Index